T0114788

The **FATHER FIGURE** "MALE OR FEMALE" COMMITMENT

Octavius Brown, LPC & LCADC

BALBOA.PRESS

A DIVISION OF HAY HOUSE

Balboa Press books may be ordered through booksellers or by contacting:

Balboa Press
A Division of Hay House
1663 Liberty Drive
Bloomington, IN 47403
www.balboapress.com
844-682-1282

Scripture quotations marked NLT are taken from the Holy Bible, New Living Translation, copyright © 1996, 2004, 2007. Used by permission of Tyndale House Publishers, Inc. Carol Stream, Illinois 60188. All rights reserved. http://www.newlivingtranslation.com/

Print information available on the last page.

ISBN: 979-8-7652-2516-5 (sc)
ISBN: 979-8-7652-2517-2 (e)

Balboa Press rev. date: 03/01/2022

PREFACE

CALLED:

I felt Called by the spirit of the LORD to author this Book. I realize that by the grace of God for seven decades, I am blessed to share my thoughts about the Glory of Unconditional Love, Forgiveness, and the importance of having as a healthy Father Figure Role Model Commitment within and outside of the Home.

Message to the Readers:

This book is ideal for couples that are planning to start a meaningful relationship or a future marriage. Similarly, will significantly help anyone that had previously experienced a divorce and is now planning their second or third marriage. Because it examines the correlation between Divorces and an unhealthy Father Figure's Commitment Role Model. That based on average second marriages results in a **sixty percent marriage Divorce Rate**. The Divorce Rates percentages are even higher for third and greater marriages.

Therefore, this is what compelled me to authoring this book. Clinically, I believe that on average people that are going or had gone through a divorce need to pause and read this book as an approach to start the process of addressing needed behavioral changes. Since coping with separation from someone you once genuinely loved is a very unhappy life experience, both parties need to recognize that a failed or failing first marriage is **strong indication** that something is wrong and needs to be clinically processed and resolved.

My hypothesis is based on my over fifty years of life experiences, numerous episodes of unregulated and unprocessed emotions, as well as an inconsistent presentation of the Father Figure's Commitment essence that was cultivated by years of embedded and unprocessed unhealthy emotions. Due to an exhibited argumentative presentation that lacked the heart of Unconditional Love and Forgiveness.

In general, regarding the connection between Divorce Rate and the Father Figure Commitment, I think, that by increasing awareness about the value of two-way healthy communication, where all parties' thoughts, feelings, and concerns are relevant. In addition, improve people passion for healthier communication within a family, will result in strengthen their readiness to implement skills to better manage unregulated emotions, resolve concerns and reduce the Divorce Rate number for second and higher marriages.

Furthermore, during the initial stages of any relationships and prior to Marriage, there should be discussions about the fundamental principles unconditional love and forgiveness. That is achieved by the implementation of effective Counseling techniques from the Nineteen Chapters in this book.

INTRODUCTION

I would like to thank you for buying my book titled The Father Figure "Male or Female" Commitment.

In the United States, as of January 2022, the most recent data from the 2019 American Community Survey put the divorces rate at 14.9 per 1,000 marriages. www.fatherly.com. This is the lowest number since 1970. However, for a person that has been previously divorced and later decides to get married again, there's a **Sixty percent chance that their marriage will fail**. www.wf-lawyers.com. The percentages are higher for the third, fourth, and other new marriages.

My hope in authoring this book is for couples to stop and take a break to look inward. They should self-reflect and research information about the long-term effects of a divorce during the children's developmental years. Divorce is serious and people must begin to recognize alternative options to discover what went wrong. This book's primary aim is to help readers learn effective techniques to reduce and better manage argumentative episodes. For the Male or Female - Father Figure, they need to process the long-term importance of their leadership within and outside the home.

After I personally have had the opportunity to self-reflect and soul search the root causes of my Divorces. I learned how challenging it is for any couple to keep their focus on the children, and be closed minded to their concerns. The Father Figure must be stable and mindful of their Father Figure Commitment role model. Because of the strong likelihood of children having serious lifelong Mental and Physical Health symptoms, the diagnoses will range from an array of Disorders like Anger Management, Self-Isolation, Academic Development, Developmental Milestones may regress, Eating and Sleeping Disorders and Anxiety Disorder are only a limited number of them. Children with Development Disorders due to the lack of having a consistent home environment, may engage in unhealthy life experiences. It is important that the Father Figure increase their awareness about why they need to avoid having a parental argumentative and unpleasant demeanor within and outside the Home.

1

DEMEANOR NEED TO BE CONSISTENT

t is my belief that Demeanor is developed during a person's developmental years from Childhood to Adulthood. The repetitive challenge is readiness to start the process of processing and resolving life experiences of trauma, grief, sorrow, mental, and physical abuse. In addition to the array of other forms of psychological or physical abuse traumas. It is these life experiences that cultivate our Demeanor.

Most unprocessed life experiences were formed from years of physical or psychological abuse from role models. If never processed, these life experiences will form the cornerstone of a person's Demeanor. Examples of an unhealthy direct life experiences are verbal argumentative conversations from a parent, teacher, or any role model. Other direct experiences are personal grief and loss, as well as academic failures due to parental or professional neglect.

The importance of learning effective techniques to begin the process of processing and resolving years of internalized embedded emotions is monumental. The therapeutic approach is started by providing a meaningful therapeutic relationship with the participant. This aids in providing a safe psychological space for the participant.

With an approachable presentation, it will enhance the participant openness to begin the Therapy Session. However, if there are periods of fluctuations, which impedes the participant's readiness, due to harmful mood shifts and sudden change to a negative demeanor. The Counselor's goal is to consistently display an approachable demeanor that emulates the therapeutic component of unconditional love.

The gift of being in the present and to express unconditional love will require the therapist to learn effective therapeutic coping skills. These skills will help the therapist to actively engage in clinical sessions that process and resolve embedded developmental life experiences. That therapeutically address the stages of the participant's Level of Change (Precontemplation, Contemplation, Preparation, Action, Maintenance, and Termination) and The Stages of Development.

The Stages of Development are Prenatal Care, Infancy through Childhood, Adolescence and Adulthood. It is during these Stages of Development that form our Demeanor.

To define each of these Stages of Development is a book by itself. Instead, I will ask you to pause and reflect on your developmental years. Then invest in at least six consecutive weeks of Counseling Sessions, with a License Professional Counselor.

The goal is to always implement healthy therapeutic techniques that helps you to consistently display an approachable DEMEANOR.

2

BAGGAGE

The 'Red Flags' in any relationship is when you witness your significant other, employer, fellow employee, friend or even a dependent overreact, as evidenced by their sudden anger outburst. Because of a statement, comment, opinion, request, or suggestion you had communicated to them. If this is a common pattern and you are starting to feel hesitant about being with them or asking, saying, or talking about something while in their presence. Due to their frequent pattern of spontaneous and unexpected exhibited anger outburst, this is a "Red Flag sign."

On a norm, the rational reason for these episodes of shown unregulated emotions, which are unknown to them, are embedded in the individual's unrefined developmental life experiences that is best known as **BAGGAGE**.

I am defining Baggage as intangible exposition of emotions (such as Hot-Button Emotions and Irrational Beliefs) that has accumulated from prior unpalatable emotional occurrences during a person's developmental years and life experiences. The psychological reoccurrences triggers are root causes of another argument that then led to the ending of one more relationship. Examples could range from ruminated thoughts about hurtful divorce emotions, or the sudden job loss due to feelings of betrayal. These nurtured deep-seated and entrenched unregulated emotions will hinder a person's openness to the glory of **Unconditional Love and Forgiveness.**

Too often, one or both individuals, within the relationship, has ingrained Baggage. Baggage that is from years of past interpersonal and social relationships life experiences. Their undigested self-deception thoughts, feelings and concerns will carry-over into their present and future relationships. The person's optimistic hope for a different outcome is artfully camouflaged by their prior relationship problem. Based on their credence that the problems were all because of the other person's faults. They believe that it was their fault because "they were" evil or vindictive. Never is there pause for them to consider the possibility that they need to address needed behavioral changes.

Self-reflection is, once again, replaced with idealistic thinking that their new relationship is going to be different because you move on to someone different. Unfortunately, the cycle returns and once again there a pattern of another Anger Management episodes of unregulated emotions, in the new relationship. While they are the same signs; however, again the individual ignores the unhealthy behavioral pattern.

The definition of insanity is **doing the same thing repeatedly and expecting a different result**. The author of these words is Albert Einstein.

Without the person's readiness to address needed behavior change their optimistic hope for a different outcome is stalled, because of their unwillingness to start the process of processing exhibited episodes of unregulated emotions. The embedded emotions are commonly labeled as Baggage. The Baggage that will consistently displayed by the person desire to bring into their next relationships, jobs, and social interactions.

What is most important is learning how to retain healthy relationships, with a special significant other, employment and other social interactions.

These are examples of how-to better address Baggage or to help increase someone's self-awareness about Baggage.

1. Take the time to deliberate on what had occurred prior to the sudden shift in emotions. Was it a disagreement, how were you feeling at the time or was it a flash back about thoughts, feelings, and concerns from an old conversation? Always, resist the impulse to reflectively get mad. **Pause to process**. Process the antecedent 2-5 minutes before this episode. Is there history of a similar episode from an earlier relationship? Is today an unhappy anniversary from a past incident of personal trauma?

   The past traumas that form as an anniversary or spoken words could trigger memories of someone special that died. Additionally, relationship separations, Divorce, sudden lifestyle abrupt change, reoccurring seasonal or common event, like the first sign of Fall or just seeing a landmark Billboard.

   Psychological it is possible for an individual's mood swing episode to be triggered by someone's body chemistry, verbal gesture, tone of voice or their demeanor. That triggers a person's reoccurring unprocessed developmental years. Years that they have nurtured stressful embedded triggers. Reoccurring triggers that are having an unproductive impact on that person's visible presentation. Furthermore, keep in mind that it is also possible for a mood swing to be a result of a familiar smell from someone's natural body odor or favorite body wash, as well as their perfume.

2. Start the process of writing down internalized unrefined thoughts, feelings and concerns that connected to undigested developmental and adult life experiences years. Schedule at least five Sessions with a Licensed Therapist

to start working on precise Anger Management Triggers and Goals.

Goal 1: Develop an effective format to track the impact of not having effective Anger Management skills.

Goal 2: Increase self-awareness on developmental and adult life experiences years that have aided their stagnation in developing effective coping skills. Skills that support a person in consistently implementing skills that emulate the concept of unconditional love.

3. Learn the value of mediation. Mediation sets the stage for learning the long-term value of relaxing the mind. With a clear mind it enables an individual to focus inwardly on thoughts, feelings, and concerns. Once concerns, feelings and thoughts are better managed then the individual needs to start to learn how to appreciate the value of productive interpersonal relationships. That then starts the process of setting up a host of meaningful corrective action plans and opportunities. This helps to enlarge your awareness to implement **of Unconditional Love and the heart of Forgiveness**.

4. Ask for feedback from your significant others, friends at work or family members. One tactful difficulty task is learning to listening. The challenge for feedback is learning to listen. This is not a time to justify, defend or challenge another individual's belief. The only way to learn is shut your mouth and listen. Without rolling your eyes or making gestures of discomfort. Stand or sit there and do one thing, listen. Listen to their belief on your Mood Swings from people that see you better than you see yourself.

If there is a need to go beyond the family members due to limited feedback, then do it. Be open to ask trusted individuals about prior social interactions. Remember that at this stage, you only need to strengthen your awareness about other people's discernment on your mood swings.

5. **Self-Inventory:** The key is your readiness to do a self-inventory by developing ways to discover anything that triggers your demeanor. An example would be is there any deviation in your demeanor during times that your significant other is socializing with their friends or making plans to attend an engagement without your presence. With the children is there a deviation in your demeanor when one child gets a particularly good school grade and another child's get a school average grade.

The art of Self-Inventory is looking in the mirror and learning to recognizing your inefficiencies. Why, on a norm people truly do not like to think about their incompetency or better status as their Level of Incompetency. Think about it, everyone has a Level of Incompetency. Therefore, the goal is learning how to compensate for that level of inherent incompetency.

When two individuals meet and there is mutual desire to start a new relationship as a couple, it is often their hope that they finally met that special person, their Soul Mate, and it was Love at first sight. During this courtship period, rarely are there any spoken awareness about prior relationships concerns or and developmental years of unprocessed as well as unresolved episodes of exhibited Mental Health Disorders.

Remember, we all have development mental health concerns. Disorders which include Bipolar Disorder, Post-Traumatic Disorder (PTSD) and Borderline Personality Disorder. Therefore, I recommend that preceding any long-term commitments, that there is a mutual agreement to actively engage in Therapy. That entails a period of consecutive active engagement Therapy Sessions, with a Licensed Mental Health Counselor. As an approach to start the slow therapeutic journey of Therapy.

Rationality for Therapy at this early stage is based on facts. It is a fraction of the future expense, in comparison to years later expenses. Expenses from repeated argumentative episodes that eventually led to ending the relationship, employment, and meaningful social interactions.

My argument is with finding the right Therapist, therapy works. The key words are **right Therapist**. People need to learn on how to trust the **Holy Spirit of Lord that is within their Soul** that is also recognized as a person's instincts.

After two to three Therapy Sessions, follow your instinct regarding if this Therapist is right for you. Because you will learn effective coping skills to aid in coping with embedded unprocessed and unresolved developmental years of mental health symptoms. Additionally, you will have started the process of learning how to uncover the developmental history that supported your mental health symptoms. Furthermore, in reference to prior relationships, there is a likelihood that your awareness about Anger Management concerns may have been the root cause of your history of break-ups. If you are convinced that your lack of coping skills to better manage unregulated emotion has been the root cause. Then through the doors of "Free Will" and with the desire to apologize for your preceding actions to former partners, social interactions, and family members, the process of healing can begin.

I thought about the best way to apologize. In which modes like emailing, texting, calling them, leaving a voice mail if unavailable or if they would want to pick-up the phone. Also, there is the choice of an in personal visit at their home. Another, possibility is to write a detailed letter and mail the letter with request for sign receipt.

The letter is to explain how therapy has helped you to evolve through self-reflection techniques. Additionally, how you now recognize the value of healthy alternative ways to better engage in a productive relationship. The letter will ask for an opportunity to seek their forgiveness with a promise to address the challenges from the prior relationship.

Over-and-above, I personally welcome the idea to ask a previous person that you had a relationship for another chance. Provide them with the details of your journey back to them and what is there about you that has changed. To retry after therapy also opens doors to other needed conversations. Yes, any new episodes will require an immediate mutual decision to pause while you return to therapy.

The choice may at times require Couple Therapy if both parties see the value in trying to address the concerns, within a therapeutic environment. Couple Therapy is a fast track in discovering the long-term value of two individuals' comparability ratio. Based on the following seven categories: Interest, Communication, Finances, Sex, Religion, Values and Morals, as well as Emphatic Heart.

The principal of self-inventory is having daily and weekly one-on-one discussions. Couples need to explore ways to better address their willingness to change. Change is key. The idea of supportive individuals actively engage in learning about the stages of change is monumental. Together they start the practice of addressing earlier blinded ideologies. That type of engagement strength the couple's awareness around showed signs of embedded unhealthy behavior patterns.

3

SELF- INVENTORY
QUESTIONS FOR COUPLES

nterest: What are the common interests? Have conversations about what are the common interests. Count the number of common interests that both parties mutually enjoy doing together and the ones doing alone. Examples do they like cooking, shopping riding a bicycle or cleaning the kitchen. Other interests are dancing, going to shows, and being with friends after work. What does one personally prefer to watch, Action Movies versus Love Movies and going dancing versus sitting at the bar? Common interests like going to a cold outdoor sporting event versus going indoor Basketball game, as well as attending a Broadway Musical Theater versus a local Movie Theater.

Communication: What are the normal topics and duration of their daily conversations? Do both parties enjoy talking about Politics, Baseball, their Profession, external family concerns and basic daily, weekly, and monthly current events? Other foundational daily topics of discussions about Personal Goals, Aims, daily life challenges, personal stories of healthy and past relationships, spiritual belief, and shared subjective opinions. Note that it is during these communication events there are opportunities to discover embedded developmental years of unprocessed and unresolved Baggage.

Finances: Do either party have problem with managing daily, weekly, and monthly finances? Are there any concerns about keeping a steady job and meeting their share of financial obligations? Are there any signs of trust concerns? Are there mutual conversations about financial obligations? Do both parties display their willingness to listen to the other person's opinion as an alternative possibility? The key about the last finance question is if their partnership in listening and processing alternative possibilities.

Sex: Do both parties genuinely enjoy their sexual interactions and the assortment of emotional and physical foreplay? Do the couples agree that foreplay makes their intimate moments an experience that they love to repeatedly achieve, over and over?

Religion: Are both believers in CHRIST? Do they respect each person's relationship with CHRIST or lack of relationship with CHRIST?

Values and Morals: When both individuals share equal sets of values and morals regardless to whether their parents raised them in church or not. As well as regardless of having different religious beliefs. The common goal is that they embrace respectful values and morals. So, the question is do both parties share similar values and morals?

Emphatic Heart: Do both express an involuntary empathic heart to care for another person or an animal?

The Decision-Making Period:

If the answers to any of these categories causes you to feel stress. Pause the relationship to Stop - Think – and then process your emotions. Reflect on your intuition as an approach to form consciousness of what you are feeling. The problem is not about who is right or wrong. It should always be about how you are feeling. It is imperative that the discussion stay on how you are feeling, about the discussion.

Furthermore, after weeks and months of healthy discussions and Therapy there are still two important questions that needs to address prior to any commitment towards the establishment of a new relationship. **First question**: Am I blinded by my innate practice of thinking "That Love Will Conquer All challenges in any committed relationship?" **Second question**: Are there natural gestures of eagerness to show a mutual respectful interpersonal relationship, as shown by, our side by sidewalk together, as equal individual in life? In life where both Individual recognizes the glory of Individuality. Individuality that defined our unique essence. Too often couples do not process the value of their Individuality.

Decision making period: If the answers to any of these categories causes you feel any anxiety. Pause the relationship. Stop and think for one to two day and then decide and schedule a date and time to share your thoughts, feelings, and concerns. Both parties must be prepared to remain rationally, without anger, while respectfully engaging in honest one-on-one conversation. The options are being in a private room and the two of you have 30 minutes to an hour discussion period. Either party could ask to reschedule and within 48 hours, make a mutually agreement on round of continued 30 minutes and one-hour sessions. Second, choice is with a mutually agreed and respected Couple Counselor. With the Couple Counselor, both parties must sign an agreement to have six consecutive sessions. Please note, there could be one to ten sets of six consecutive Couple Counseling Sessions. Third choice is weekly Individual and one Couple Session, each, or every other week.

The goal for Therapy and One-on-One Discussions, **is to process the other person's internalized thoughts, feelings, and concerns with each other**. This process could help couples reflect on their intuition in an effective and healthy manner. Once again, this process is not about who is right or wrong. It is an opportunity to listen and process the other person's emotions. Once a partner is finished, share your understanding of what they are sharing and in a respectful manner than share your thoughts, feelings, and concerns.

4

TIME-OUT

All Family Members must have mutual capability to call a "Time-Out." Once spoken, all Family Members that are within the sound of their voice, must stop whatever they were doing. To listen to whatever that person, who is calling "Time-Out," needs to say.

Family Members responsibility is to confirm their thoughts, feelings, and concerns. Also, this is an alternative way to schedule an abrupt Family Meeting. This privilege is a means to ease internalized thoughts, feelings, and concerns.

This re-occurring practice may be a means to better manage daily, weekly, and monthly family stressful obligations within and outside of the home. That will also nurture healthy role model behavior patterns towards children, social, and professional interactions. Additionally, support parents and role-models need to be cognizance of a family member early signs of mental and physical health symptoms.

Further, this approach helps to bring into focus problems that are originating outside the home. Examples are a family member's "must get done" project for school or job. Stressful interpersonal relationships at work, as shown by, a boss or an ongoing unhealthy interaction at school, neighborhood or at work.

The Time-out option is an approach to gain family members' awareness of a sudden uncommonly behavior pattern about someone within family. Therefore, based on their insight, regarding concerns of a family member mental or physical health symptoms. They have the right to request a "Time Out."

The choice is also for when children are having unsound interactions with peers at school that is having a negative effect on their grades. Additionally, occasions of where a family member reported harassment episodes by someone or group of individuals students at school. Another, example is if a parent or role-model within the family is too preoccupied with someone or something outside of the home that results in little to no attention to someone within the home. To summarize, any situations that causes individuals within the family to feel invisible and symptoms of neglect.

In my immediate family the distraction for me was that I worked too much, as evidence by two full time jobs during the week and then working 32 hours on the weekend. This type of tunnel vision resulted in my inability to truly acknowledge my three daughters. Today, I would trade all my monetary gains for those lost precious moments I missed during my children early childhood developmental stages and other precious period of their development.

Therefore, Parents must keep their priorities in order. To better embrace the importance of checking-in daily or weekly or monthly with their children. The point is developing a habit of checking-in. While family members continue the pattern of nurturing each other's thoughts, feelings, and concerns. Once again, all family members will need to feel welcome to speak the words, Time-Out. Because these two words, within their family, will result in family member's involuntary and non-judgmental action to Stop. Stop to listen to their brother or sister's concern. The topic of discussion is not about who is right or wrong. What is significance is the dependable and heart felt empathic display of only being focused on that person's belief.

Using my parents as an example. Both parents implemented parenting tactics that, today's standard, is Child Abuse. However, both were truly enthusiastic about their way of parenting. It appears to me that neither parent ever thought about the generational harm, known as the Generational Curse. According to the Gospel Coalition, a "generational curse describes the cumulative effect on a person or things that their ancestors did, believed, or practiced in the past, and a consequence of an ancestor's actions, beliefs, and sins being passed down."

During their generation children were never taught on how to share or express thoughts, feelings, and concerns. Instead, their expectation was only to obey and listen to what their parent or elder was asking them to do. However, the improvement in modern-day cultures is based in the States Human Service Departments.

The Therapist challenge is to increase parent's readiness to willfully "break the generational curse." To be open to address needed behavior changes and avoid the pattern of not taken the time to listen to their children. To achieve this, parents must first acknowledge the concept of **The Generational Curse** and then their willingness to implement needed parental behavior changes towards their children.

To change, is a process. Families must develop a better understanding about the importance of sharing internalizing thoughts, feelings, and concerns in a healthy and respectful manner. In addition, as parents the role is to start the process of strengthening their children awareness about the importance of learning healthier communicate skills to best internalized emotions in a rational and respectful manner.

One of the many Courses parents and family members should enroll in is Anger Management. This Course would help family members start the process of implementing effective Anger Management techniques. All mature family members must complete the therapeutic Anger Management Course, prior to processing the concept of The Generational Curse, within a family.

In 1986, my family and I were living in a three-bedroom home in the Bronx, NY. Theresa was pregnant with Jennifer, at the time. My brilliant plan is a perfect example of how I had 100% tunnel vision. The plan was to give the soon to be newborn baby Octavia's room. Octavia have had that room for the past 6 years. Total tunnel vision.

What wrong is that I only focused on the baby needs and never once had a second thoughts about Octavia's needs. Now it is as clear as a sunny morning sunrise. I am sure Octavia had many unhappy thoughts, feelings, and concerns about her privacy being taken away. Especially, without having even one discussion about her thoughts. In addition, it probable that both daughters Cassandra and Octavia had unspoken concerns, regarding the loss of their privacy. What is most troubling, at the time, I was financially stable to purchase a large home. Because, I had discretionary family income to move the Family into a four- or five-Bedroom home.

I proceeded forward without one conversation or any type of a meaningful discussion with either of my daughters and wife. Never had one discussion about Octavia being moved into her sister Cassandra's room. Also, never once did it ever dawn to me, to have a conversation with Octavia and Cassandra or ask for their opinion about my great idea of changing their living arraignment. This would have been an excellent time for a "Time Out."

My serious mental health issues prevented me from processing their disappointment due to my deficiency in the Art of Effective Listening Skills and not having any Family format in place for anyone in the Family to say Time-Out. Now, after at least 10 years of Mental Health training, it is clear to me that I was wrong.

Now, I understand how my "Great Plan" was one example of how I caused both of my daughters to experience the feeling of neglect. The reason is that the concept of "TIME-OUT" was never an option. Neither daughter ever had the right to say "TIME-OUT."

A chance to share their thoughts, feelings, and concerns about losing their independence of having their own bedroom.

Exercise: Have a conversation with you Family regarding one of the Father Figure's "Great Idea" that occurred without any of the children's input.

In reference to my very minor defense that based on my lack of awareness, is a very moot point. The reason is my childhood developmental years. Just the thought of maintaining or even having some type of Level of Independence or autonomy was never an option or an active thought. While living at my parent's home. I never had my own room or bed. Furthermore, I never experienced any prior awareness or notion of having a meaningful two-way conversation with either one of my parents. Never were there an opportunity to share heartfelt thoughts, feelings, and concerns to either of my parents, because of their ingrained concept of one-way communication. That was their way and as their children, we are to do what we are told to do. Which, I unfortunately brought into my family.

I grew-up in a three bedrooms apartment. One room was for my parents, another was for Anthony and Tommy and the third room, was for me, Vincent, and Larry. Besides having to share the room, we also had to share the one bed. Anthony and Tommy had their own bed but slept in the same room.

Therefore, I am strongly advocating, if possible, that each child should or need to have their own room. To achieve the beginning level of responsibility of learning to keep their room clean and in order. Yes, it would also be helpful for our children to start the process of developing their independence in combination with their identity and personal likes and dislike.

What I am suggesting is that each child must never sense the feeling of being neglected. Instead, they must be reassured about feeling safe within their home to share thoughts, feelings, concerns, regarding school, likes and dislikes and stress in a Safe and Constructive manner. Children must always feel safe and absolute that their parents have a genuine desire to listen to their concerns. They must recognize that there will be times of disagreements; however they must always welcome the privilege to engage in healthy non-argumentative conversations.

With a compassionate heart, Parents need to encourage children to feel safe in sharing their internalized emotions within the boundaries of their home, school, and neighborhood. Therefore, I am suggesting that The Father Figure's role-models encourage the Time-Out concept, as an approach to develop the children willingness to share their emotions, in a healthy therapeutic manner.

The "Time-Out" concept should start as early at the age of five years old. Family Meetings should be a common event within the Family. The Father Figure role-models need to experience the glory of having healthy discussions, as each person's opinion is discussed in a respectful manner. Likewise, Parents need to promote opportunities for Family Meetings to discuss the reason/purpose of asking for a Family Member request for a "Time-Out." Explain and develop Family Rules about ways to share emotions in a healthy manner versus unhealthy manner like an anger outburst due to occasions of having unregulated internalized emotions.

Another example from my life experiences is regarding the important to learning the concept of "Time-Out" at least within your immediate Family.

In 1972, Anthony and I started an Import and Export Store on Courtland Ave, Bronx, New York, between East 153 Street and East 154 Street. The Store was right across from where we lived. We named the business Brown's Brothers. We had a connection with imports from Kenya Africa that sold us African items like Canes, Dashiki, African, Zebra skins rugs, and African wooden Figures.

In addition, to support a steady cash flow we sold cigarettes and other products that were normally sold at the local Pharmacy Store.

The point in bringing up this example is about the Time-Out suggestion. With the Time-Out option, I think we may have found an alternative solution to address the Store's burglary problem versus closing the store. The decision to close was based on us having several burglary incidents that occurred during closing and at night, between the hour of 1 AM to 5AM.

Once I received the call, that the store had been burglarized, I would run down to the store. On one occasion, I remember arriving at the store and looking at how they broke-in through the walls or bottom front of the store. The next morning, I decided to start keeping my dogs in the store at night. Within a brief period, our stock was replaced apart from the imported items from Kenya. Once back-up and ready to open for business, it did not take long for it to happen again. The Brown's Brother Store had another burglary. The last burglary brought on a sense of defeat. Therefore, after a conversation between Anthony and I, the Brown Brothers' Store was closed.

Imagine, if we had the "Time-Out" practice response versus the defeated posture. I honestly believe that a Time-Out would have better prepared us in coping with the daily challenges of business and life.

I could go on and on with "What if" examples like: Once the words, (Time Out), were spoken and we (brothers from oldest to youngest were Leonard/Tommy, Anthony, Vincent, myself, and Larry) all had the foresight to pause and listen to each other and adopted the true value of establishing a meaningful Family Discussion. "What if" my mother, (Essie), who was wheelchair bound due to MS, taught the Time-Out concept to us and other parents and children within the South Bronx neighborhood? Last, "What if," my father (Octavius) that had to work two jobs to support a family of five boys, had learned how to use and practice the Time-Out concept? Furthermore, if my father had been taught The Father Figure Role Models concept during their developmental years and then display why it is important to share internalized emotions.

My developmental life experiences are rooted in a generation that only taught children how to obey the parents. Never, was it about how to address our feelings of neglect, depression, anger, and any concerns that were rooted from within or outside of the family.

From my perspective, society will benefit by the achievement of efficient social interaction skills, if "Time-Out" was taught in school and home as an opportune approach toward the long- term achievement of Critical Thinking. In addition, as an approach to venting unregulated emotions, thoughts, feelings, and concerns in a receptive manner.

Consequently, I am hoping that the future generations to pick-up the mantle for Time-Out. To use this tool as process for learning healthier decision-making skills, within and outside of the home. Skills that embrace the concepts of calling a "Time-Out" as an effective approach in reducing our children's anxieties and ruminations of unfruitful and unregulated emotions. Instead, Teach the concept of "Time-Out" in schools and within the home. Once again, if taught correctly, it is the opportune approach towards the long-term achievement of developing our brothers and sisters Critical Thinking ability.

5

SCHEDULE MEETINGS

Schedule Meetings: Have scheduled meetings with family to process internalized emotions or any other concerns.

The Importance of FAMILY MEETINGS

It is my belief that the Family is the single most important influence in a child's life. From the very first moments of life, children depend on parents and family to **protect them and support their needs**. Parents are a child's first teachers and function as their role models in showing them how to act and how to experience the world around them.

Reference **www.smartbeginningsmhc.org**

The Father Figure must be laser focus on how a healthy Family should function. The Family actions are paramount during a child's developmental years as well as the period following the onset of puberty during which a young person develops from a child into an adult, the adolescence stage of their maturity.

Parents must understand that there is "No Do Over" regarding the years that set the stages for children's phases of development. Parents decisions must be done with healthy exhibited consistency and clarity, as they address the Child's developmental requirements.

Family Meeting:

On a norm a Family Meeting should be at least once a month. The format needs to be constant as possible regarding the time and duration of each Meeting. In addition, there need to be designated individuals for the many different tasks like sending out the link for the meeting, collecting the topics and making the arraignment for the order of discussions, prior to the date and time of the Meeting. The clear objective is for family members to come together, as one body, for meaningful conversation about a one or several family members or personal concern with individuals that genuinely care about their thoughts and wellness, within a safe environment of family love.

During times when there minimum to any concerns about someone within the family, then it may be ideal that meetings are every other month. In comparison to times of concerns like one of the parents' health, or if an individual is having an adverse encounter with somebody and would like to receive family members encouraging feedback versus judgment.

We would all agree that everyone is born into a family, but not everyone gets a healthy/functional Family. For those who are not privileged to have a healthy birth family, they often create a chosen family later. Why is family important? What kind of impact does it have on a person in their childhood and as an adult? Does it matter to society as a whole? Here are ten reasons that will help answer the prior questions and why family is important:

1. Families set the stage for future relationships:

    The very first relationships a child has is with their parents and any siblings. Whether functional or dysfunctional relationships supply a model for what future relationships will look like. It is often not a conscious decision, but for better or worse, people often choose partners and friends based on how similar they are to their family. Family dynamics repeat themselves and reinforce beliefs about relationships and self.

2. During challenging times, people need a family they can rely on:

   When life gets hard, people need support. This can be emotional and/or financial support. Someone going through rough times will turn to their family if they trust them to provide encouragement and love. Feeling accepted and understood during a personal crisis is a basic need for people. Families – whether traditional or chosen – can provide that.

3. Families can be an essential source of affection and encouragement:

   In good or tough times, the family need to supply affection and encouragement. At times, it can be difficult to find friends or purpose in adulthood. If a person has a strong family, they will always be able to find the love and support they need. With their family behind them, a person will find the motivation and courage for success. On the other side, if a person is not getting love and support from a family structure, they will feel lonely, depressed, and even hopeless.

4. Families foster a sense of belonging to something greater than oneself:

   Families are hubs of tradition. Also, families continue traditions through the years by sharing stories from the past. This creates <u>connections with family members</u> that aren't around anymore. A person who grows up in this type of family feels like they belong to something bigger than themselves. They will take pride in being a member of a community that has gone through hardships and triumphs.

5. People raised in close families develop healthier relationships throughout their lives:

    <u>Research</u> supports that people from close-knit families go on to enjoy close relationships later in life. *Psychological Science* published a long-running study in 2016 that looked at men's relationships. Researchers learned that men who grew up in nurturing families developed stronger relationships than men who did not have accepting families. They managed their emotions well and kept a closer connection with their partners.

6. Family relationships are linked to a person's mental health:

    There have been many studies on the importance of family <u>time</u>, specifically dinner time. While families can still be healthy even if they do not eat dinner together every night, there is a correlation between this time together and a young person's wellbeing. In *Pediatrics*, one study discovered that kids who ate with their families regularly were less likely to show depression symptoms. On the other side of the spectrum, research shows that negative family relationships can trigger or worsen mental health issues.

7. Quality time with family is linked to better academic performance:

   The National Center on Addiction and Substance Abuse at Columbia University conducted a series of studies on family dinner time. One study showed that kids who eat dinner with their family less than three times were twice as likely to get Cs or below in school. On the other hand, kids who had family dinners 5-7 times a week did much better. Of course, there are other factors at play, but families that value dinners together likely value other positive family interactions.

8. Families teach important life lessons.

   Families are the first place where children learn how to manage their emotions, interact with others, and communicate. It is also the first setting where kids learn about consequences, either positive or negative. Parents will need to form a bold with their children for developing plans to manage their life experiences for them to remember for years to come. These lessons form a big part of a person's worldview and on how they believe the world works.

9. Families teach values:

   Along with life lessons, people learn a value system within their family structure. They learn what their family defines as right or wrong, as well as what is important to the community. These values become ingrained and form a foundational part of a person's identity. Values affect how a person treats others, how they view themselves, and what they see as their purpose in life.

10. Healthy families form the backbone of a healthy society:

> When families are strong, communities are strong. That naturally leads to a strong society. The definition of a "healthy" or "good" is often the subject of heated debate. Countless studies have explored the impacts of adoption, LGBTQ+ relationships, families with multiple ethnicities, and so on. Why? Society is deeply invested in the strength of families because there is a domino effect. If families are not doing well, a nation will suffer. If families are happy and healthy, the nation benefits.

https://theimportantsite.com/10-reasons-family-is-important

My hope is that this Chapter strengthen individuals' compassion towards showing ways to nourish their family members awareness about why you need each other. Using the common concept about the word Team, where as your Family is the Team: That there is no I in Team. I am saying Family members need to stop thinking that their life decision-making will only affect them.

The choice of coming together as a Family is what we need. No child needs to feel alone and think isolation thoughts. We are not on our own island because we were born into a family. If it a healthy family that great, if not, we must make the best out of an unpleasant situation, by finding a Family that you would like to emulate. Within the structure of a Family Meeting, that aim is to help to reduce your stress and brings you to that greatest posture. The posture that helps you cope and better manage with the daily challenges of life.

6

PHYSICAL THERAPY

I n reference to children, during their developmental years, **Physical Therap**y can be very productive in improving their balance, strength, and motor skills. If your **child** is missing physical milestones (an action or event marking a meaningful change or stage in their development), you **should** consider the choice of scheduling them for an appointment to meet with their primary Doctor.

Recommended pediatric *physical therapy* helps *children* learn to perform gross motor skills and functional mobility skills successfully and independently. It also, helps young athletes in learning to implement effective techniques to prevent and better manage an injury by addressing any muscle imbalance or weakness as well as help them to return to play after an injury. Reference napacenter.org April 15, 2021.

Physical Therapy Guide to Developmental Delay

Developmental delay describes the behavior of young children whose development in key mental and physical areas is slower than other children of the same age. The delay can be in any areas of development, such as movement (motor control), speaking, thinking, playing, or self-care skills.

It has been estimated that 14% of all toddlers and preschoolers in the United States are classified as having developmental delay.

However, about 1 in 4 children through the age of five are at risk for a developmental delay or disability. Early identification allows communities to start the process of an effective and affordable treatment during the preschool years and can lessen the need for expensive special-education services in later childhood.

Reference Pediatrics October 2019 (https: doi.org/10.1542/peds.2019-0811)

OBJECTIVES: To study the national prevalence of ten developmental disabilities in US children aged 3 to 17 years and explore changes over time by associated demographic and socioeconomic characteristics, using the National Health Interview Survey.

METHODS: Data come from the 2009 to 2017 National Health Interview Survey (NHIS), a nationally representative survey of the civilian noninstitutionalized population. Parents reported physician or other health care professional diagnoses of attention-deficit/hyperactivity disorder; autism spectrum disorder; blindness; cerebral palsy; moderate to profound hearing loss; learning disability; intellectual disability; seizures; stuttering or stammering; and other developmental delays. Weighted percentages for each of the selected developmental disabilities and any developmental disability were calculated and stratified by demographic and socioeconomic characteristics.

RESULTS: From 2009 to 2011 and 2015 to 2017, there were overall significant increases in the prevalence of developmental disability (16.2%–17.8%, $P < .001$), attention-deficit/hyperactivity disorder (8.5%–9.5%, $P < .01$), autism spectrum disorder (1.1%–2.5%, $P < .001$), and intellectual disability (0.9%–1.2%, $P < .05$), but a significant decrease for any other developmental delay (4.7%–4.1%, $P < .05$). The prevalence of any developmental disability increased among boys, older children, non-Hispanic white and Hispanic children, children with private insurance only, children with birth weight ≥2500 g, and children living in urban areas and with less-educated mothers.

CONCLUSIONS: The prevalence of developmental disability among US children aged 3 to 17 years increased between 2009 and 2017. Changes by demographic and socioeconomic subgroups may be related to improvements in awareness and access to health care.

Abbreviations:

> ADHD — *Attention Deficit/Hyperactivity Disorder*
> ASD — *Autism Spectrum Disorder*
> CP — *Cerebral Palsy*
> FPL — *Federal Poverty Level*
> ID — *Intellectual Disability*
> LD — *Learning Disability*
> NHIS — *National Health Interview Survey*
> NSCH — *National Survey of Children's Health*

RESULTS

Prevalence

Between 2009 and 2017, the overall prevalence of developmental disability among children aged 3 to 17 years in the United States was 16.93%, ranging from 0.16% for blindness to 9.04% for ADHD.

Child-Level Characteristics

Overall, children in the oldest age group (ages 12–17 years) were the most likely to be diagnosed with developmental disability and specifically with ADHD, LD, and ID; however, they were least likely to be diagnosed with stuttering or stammering or other developmental delay and less likely to be diagnosed with seizures than children aged 3 to 5 years. Boys were more likely than girls to be diagnosed with developmental disability, specifically with ADHD, ASD, CP, LD, ID, stuttering or stammering, and other developmental delay.

Non-Hispanic white children were most likely to be diagnosed with ADHD and more likely to be diagnosed with ASD than non-Hispanic Black or Hispanic children. Non-Hispanic Black children were most likely to be diagnosed with LD, stuttering, or stammering. Hispanic children were least likely to be diagnosed with ADHD. Overall, non-Hispanic white and non-Hispanic Black children were more likely to be diagnosed with developmental disability when compared with either non-Hispanic other children or Hispanic children.

Children receiving any form of public health insurance were more likely to be diagnosed with each of the individual developmental disabilities when compared with children receiving only private health insurance and uninsured children, except for blindness in the latter group. Children with only private health insurance were more likely to be diagnosed with ADHD, ASD, and any other developmental delay when compared with uninsured children but were less likely to be diagnosed with LD. Children with low birth weight (<2500 g) were more likely to be diagnosed with any and each of the specific developmental disabilities when compared with children of normal birth weight.

Family-Level Characteristics

Children with mothers who had a college or greater education level were least likely to be diagnosed with any developmental disability and specifically least likely to be diagnosed with LD, ID, seizures, and stuttering or stammering. Children with mothers with less than a high school education were more likely to be diagnosed with blindness, LD, ID, or stuttering or stammering but were less likely to be diagnosed with ADHD or any other developmental delay when compared with children with mothers who had only completed high school or levels of colleges.

Children in families living at <200% of the FPL were more likely to have been diagnosed with each developmental disability, except ASD. Children with a rural residence compared with an urban residence were significantly more likely to be diagnosed with any developmental disability conditions, including ADHD, hearing loss, and LD.

Time Trends

The prevalence of any developmental disability increased significantly (16.22%–17.76%; an increase of 9.5%), comparing the years 2009 to 2011 to 2015 to 2017. During this period, significant increases were also observed for ADHD (8.47%–9.54%; an increase of 12.6%), ASD (1.12%–2.49%; an increase of 122.3%), and ID (0.93%–1.17%; an increase of 25.8%), but a significant decrease was seen for the category of "other developmental delay" (4.65%–4.06%; a decrease of 12.7%).

Demographic and Socioeconomic Characteristics

Between 2009 and 2017, there was a significant increase seen in the prevalence of any developmental disabilities for the oldest children (ages 12–17 years), boys, non-Hispanic white and Hispanic children, children with private insurance only, and children with normal birth weight. An increase in prevalence was also seen for children living with mothers who had a high school or college level of education, children living in families in both FPL groups, and children living in urban areas. Also, with children that had low birth weight, children living with mothers who have less than a high school education, and children living in rural areas and were not statistically significant, perhaps because of smaller sample sizes for these subgroups.

Discussion

Overall, ~1 in 6 children (~17%) between the ages of 3 to 17 in the United States were reported to have a developmental disability diagnosis between 2009 and 2017. During this eight-year period, there was a significant increase in the overall rate of developmental disabilities, largely because of increases in the prevalence of ADHD, ASD, and ID, but with a concomitant decrease in the prevalence of "any other developmental delay."

ADHD

The increase in prevalence of diagnosed ADHD among US children and adolescents since the late 1990s has been well documented, although there is evidence that the prevalence of ADHD symptoms and impairment has remained steady over time. Taken together, this suggests that the increases in diagnosed prevalence could be driven by better identification of children who meet criteria for ADHD, as current estimates of diagnosed prevalence are in line with community-based studies in which researchers measured symptoms and impairment against *Diagnostic and Statistical Manual of Mental Disorders* diagnostic criteria. The American Academy of Pediatrics published updated guidelines in 2011 for the diagnosis and treatment of ADHD, which may have influenced diagnostic practices over the study period. Availability of treatment may also be related to increases in the diagnosis of ADHD, as there are effective pharmacologic and nonpharmacologic treatments that have been and continue to be developed to address ADHD symptoms and associated negative functioning.

ASD

The reported prevalence of ASD in the United States and other industrialized countries has shown marked increases in recent decades. However, understanding changes to ASD prevalence is still particularly challenging given that the diagnosis of ASD is based on a symptom profile, and health care provider and school practices for ASD screening, diagnosis, and classification continue to evolve. Nonetheless, a sizable part of the ASD prevalence increase is explained by improved identification of children with ASD related to increasing parental awareness and changing provider practices, including universal screening by 18 to 24 months and ongoing monitoring of a child's development as recommended by the American Academy of Pediatrics in 2007.

Although not directly assessed in the current study, changes in diagnostic criteria and reporting practices have been associated with increases in the number of "catch-up" diagnoses seen in older children. In fact, results from the National Survey of Children's Health (NSCH) documented that much of the observed prevalence increase reported in each successive survey was explained by diagnoses in older children within given birth cohorts. The composition of children with ASD has also changed over the years, with the co-occurrence of ID decreasing in recent years, a result of broadening diagnostic criteria.

Finally, changes in the prevalence of ASD as measured by the NHIS may also be tied to survey measurement. An increase of ~80% was seen in the 2014 NHIS following changes to the wording and ordering of the question capturing ASD. Future wording changes may be needed to align the ASD question with *Diagnostic and Statistical Manual of Mental Disorders, Fifth Edition* criteria.

ID

In the NHIS, the increase in the prevalence of ID also appears to coincide with changes to the wording or ordering of survey questions. ID prevalence was relatively stable between 1997 and 2008 when the survey asked about "mental retardation" but was 72% higher in 2011 to 2013 when the question asked about "intellectual disability, also known as mental retardation."[7] It has been hypothesized that wording changes may have decreased social desirability pressures (e.g., parents may be more comfortable endorsing ID rather than mental retardation) while increasing the ability to recognize and correctly endorse the condition by including both terms.

Other Developmental Delay

"Other developmental delay" was the only condition to show a statistically significant decrease over time. It is possible that parents have become less likely to select this category because their children have increasingly been diagnosed with another specified condition on the survey. Evidence supporting this type of "diagnostic substitution" has been shown previously in special education administrative data sets.

Demographic and Socioeconomic Characteristics

Patterns related to diagnosed developmental disabilities by child-level and family-level characteristics were largely similar to those found in previous studies, with a higher prevalence of any developmental disabilities and specific disorders for boys, older children, children whose birth weight was lower than 2500 g, non-Hispanic white children, children with public insurance, children with mothers with less than a college education, and children living in a household <200% of the federal poverty line.

The higher prevalence of identified disorders among children living in rural areas may be related to differences in demographic patterns and risk factors in rural areas, including greater financial difficulties and less access to amenities and treatment resources. The overall difference between urban and rural prevalence can primarily be attributed to discrepancies seen for behavioral conditions, such as ADHD and LD. In earlier research, authors have named notable rural behavioral health barriers, such as lack of access to transportation and availability of specialized providers who prevent and treat symptoms of these conditions. Meanwhile, ADHD, ID, and LD were also more prevalent among older children than younger children, which may reflect that these diagnoses might not be formally recognized until a child is in school.

Overall, the general consistency of demographic patterns with earlier studies, particularly suggests that underlying, contributing factors, such as service availability, continue to be associated with the prevalence of developmental disabilities. These same demographic subgroups that had higher prevalence of any developmental disabilities were also the groups that showed significant increases from 2009 to 2011 to 2015 to 2017.

Strengths and Limitations

The NHIS has notable strengths in both its large sample size and high response rate for a national survey, allowing for analysis among subgroups of children with less common developmental disabilities. The NHIS provides prompt and in-depth information on the health conditions, service use, and family sociodemographic characteristics of children with developmental disabilities. Estimates produced from the NHIS interpretation as nationally representative when weight and the complex survey design variables are implemented in an analysis, supplying powerful evidence of the proportion and number of noninstitutionalized children affected by developmental disabilities in the United States.

Despite these strengths, caution called for because of survey-related limitations. First, in instances, statistical trend tests may have been underpowered because of smaller sample sizes (e.g., rural residents). Second, the reliance on parent report could result in the misreporting of children's diagnoses because these reports may also be subject to recall biases, particularly among parents of older children. Thirdly, there was no mechanism in place to confirm parent-reported diagnoses either through clinical evaluation or educational records. However, there is notable consistency between results of the NHIS and other nationally representative surveys, including the NSCH. Recent, population based ASD estimates have found to be virtually identical when comparing ASD prevalence in the 2016 NSCH and the 2016 NHIS. A broader comparison of a select set of developmental disabilities (including ASD) with comparable question wordings between multiple iterations of the NSCH and the NHIS produced comparable findings suggesting further evidence of convergent validity.

Caution should typically be when comparing published prevalence estimates derived from different surveillance systems and surveys with varying rigor of case ascertainment. However, it is worth noting that survey-based estimates from both the NHIS and the NSCH have fallen within the range of estimates provided by the Centers for Disease Control and Prevention's Autism and Developmental Disabilities Monitoring Network, particularly when aligned with a comparable age group, suggesting a degree of consistency.

Finally, as parents are reporting on a lifetime diagnosis, it is likely that children included in the current analysis no longer have a diagnosable developmental disability. It is known that the persistence of developmental disabilities is highly variable by condition, with children losing a diagnosis because of maturation or the ability to effectively manage their condition.

Conclusions:

The percentage of children diagnosed with a developmental disability increased significantly between 2009 and 2017, resulting in a growing population of children (~1 out of every 6) with 1 or more developmental disabilities. Given this growth, other research may help to better understand the characteristics of children with developmental disabilities, the complex risk factors associated with developmental disabilities, and the accessibility of services and interventions, which have shown to improve long-term outcomes for those diagnosed with a developmental disability.

Furthermore, Children who have problems that inhibit their movement development also may develop a fear of trying new motor skills, which can then lead to social or emotional problems.

7

MENTAL HEALTH COUNSELING

Top 5 Reasons to Consult with a Mental Health Professional (Eric D. Caine, M.D.www.urmc.rochester.edu)

A good place to begin your research for an excellent Mental Health Professional is to seek the advice of your primary care physician, who is aware of local mental health colleagues. Remember, we all have development mental health concerns. Therefore, early help for a mental health issue can make an enormous difference.

- The first reason is when you have thoughts, emotions or behaviors that are out of control, especially when they are affecting your social interactions at work or sense of well-being. Never feel embarrassed to ask for help at times when you are upset or depressed.
- Next is when you are struggling to deal with life's painful challenges – such as a major illness, the loss of a loved one, divorce or job problems. These issues may be your own but could also include those of others you care about.
- The third is when the use of alcohol or drugs interferes with your health, emotions, social interactions with your significant other, children, community relationships, employment interactions and your ability to fulfill daily responsibilities within the home.
- Another is when you are confused, fraught with unhealthy ruminating unregulated emotions and need the

perspectives of a caring yet unbiased person to help sort among difficult choices.

- And lastly, when you feel that life is no longer worth living, that you are hopeless and have reached the end of the line, and you would rather die than feel the pain of the present. During such distress, you are not prepared to make life-or-death decisions. This is the time to ask for immediate help.

8

PREMARITAL COUNSELING

I strongly believe that my child, adolescence, and adult years of unprocessed and unhealthy developmental years, as well as my inconsistent pattern of mimicking The Father Figure Commitment Role Model presentation played a negative factor in each of my three marriages that resulted in divorce. Now I realize why.

I failed to pause and then start the process of self-reflection. Instead, I took comfort in ruminating on internalized Baggage that entailed unhealthy thoughts, feelings, and concerns regarding my past dysfunctional life experiences. In addition, throughout my marriages, I displayed bare minimum appreciation regarding the important of my wife's individuality. In other words, I never process the value of my wife's individuality. Never once did I recognize or acknowledged their unique quality and the things that distinguishes them from others. Furthermore, I did not display The Father Figure Commitment Role Model as evidenced by the following eight requirements:

1. Maintain Laser focus on ways to emulate Unconditional Love
2. Consistently practice the art of Forgiveness
3. Recognize the value of our Individuality
4. Practice the Art of Constructive Criticism
5. Practice the Art of Effective Listening Skills

6. Take time to research for a Professional Therapist (That practice Premarital Counseling. It is vital that both parties feels that special sense of rapport with the Therapist. Therefore, validate that both parties are comfortable and sense a rapport. If not, please continue researching. This is the most crucial phase of attending PREMARITAL COUNSELING)

7. Share internalized emotions with someone you trust

8. Practice the comfort in praying and leaving it at the Altar

It is my belief, that if I had taken the time to do any one of these eight requirements, there is a strong likelihood that I would still be in my first marriage. In comparison to being in the greater than sixty percentage or greater Divorce Category. In thinking about it even further, there would not have been a second marriage, because all the concerns about the first marriage would had been resolved.

Now, at this stage of my life, I could only imagine the better outcome for all parties, if we took the time to invest in attending a Professional Pre-Marital Counselor, during the preliminary stages of our relationship and while we were planning to get married.

It is possible that both parties' happiness would have been better if we had the foresight to seek a **mutually agreed-upon** Professional Marital Counselor, at least 6 months, prior to the wedding.

Couples will need to believe that it is a must, not an option. They need to schedule Pre-Marital Counseling Sessions with a mutually agreed-upon Professional Marital Counselor. At least, 6 months prior to the wedding date. This approach is to help couples start the conversation of each person's expectations. In addition, it is to start the process of processing concerns in a more thought-out professional manner. Furthermore, this would be the time to have a detail discussion regarding the Father Figure Commitment Role Model within and outside of the home.

Furthermore, I am also recommending that each person schedule, at least six one-on-one therapeutic sessions with the Counselor, as an approach to address their early, Adolescence and Adult Developmental years of entrench baggage.

In my case I unknowingly carried baggage into each of my three marriages. That negatively had an adverse effect that resulted in each of marriage ending in a divorce. I genuinely believe it was because in each marriage. I never once took the time to process my early childhood, adolescent, and adult embedded developmental years of Baggage. Additionally, never once did I look in the mirror. To see how I lacked the readiness to embrace the glory of the Lord, and emulated Unconditional Love with an empathic heart and fortify bridge to Forgiveness.

Consequently, now I am aware of the power of forgiveness and God's Agape Love.

9

THE ART OF CONSTRUCTIVE CRITICISM

The Art of Constructive Criticism

I will assess that on a norm, most people do not appreciate criticism. Learning the Art of Constructive Criticism with help to ease the process. My goal is to explain Ten Techniques on how best to administer constructive criticism. To begin, I plan to discuss how to teach someone to accept constructive criticism.

1. It is extremely important never to display unhealthy facial expressions when you are criticizing an individual.
2. Always implement healthy listening skills that display attentiveness to the person that is talking.
3. On occasions while the person is speaking acknowledge them with the OK or I understand.
4. Be mindful of ways to minimize the problem. If you are asked to do something, do it if you are asked to stop to do something stop it.
5. Describe the problem using at descriptive statement instead of language with that can be perceived as judgmental. There is no point in being judgmental because it will only worsen the situation. Therefore, use language that recognize their efforts and then supportive feedback as an approach to be part of the solution to rectify the problem.

6. Prior to any criticizing, do your best research to discover the root of the problem. Work with the individual to gather information about what are the causes of the problem, as well as alternative solutions to address or by a process of eliminations. In addition, this is a major opportunity to jointly implement effective critical thinking skills, together.

7. Always implement healthy anger management skills as an approach to never allow anger or unregulated emotions to enter your conversations. No one likes hearing criticism in an unsympathetic attitude. Prior to any constructive criticism discussion, confirm that your emotions and level of annoyance is not a concern. If there is a presence of unregulated emotions, wait until your temper has "calm-down." Do the following: Breathe, admit that you are anxious, challenge your emotions, Release the anxiety by listening to music or taking a walk to think things through.

8. In an empathic manner communicate your thoughts about the consequences of their inaccuracy and misstep.

9. Before you decide to criticism anyone make sure that your information as factual. Also, prior to criticizing someone, make sure you know what and how you plan to communicate your thoughts, feelings, and concerns in a healthy manner. The aim is to educate versus embarrassment.

10. The goal of constructive criticism is to prompt an individual to realize that there is an opportunity to improve their changes towards known goals and expectations.

In conclusion, it is importance to understand that the Art of Constructive Criticism is a valuable tool to comfort someone in a non-defensive manner. It is my hopes that you will learn how to use this technique in a non-vindictive, non-self-interest and unharmful demeanor. For the love of decency, we all should use this tool to elevate our brothers and sisters. The glory is in building versus tearing down anyone of our brothers and sisters. Therefore, we should always try to practice effective ways to implement The Art of Constructive Criticism in an unconditional loving and forgiving manner.

10

THE ART OF EFFECTIVE LISTENING

How to develop the Art of Effective Listening

In any one-on-one conversation or being in the audience when someone is speaking, will require having effective listening skills. The dilemma for people with poor listening skills will range from a language barrier, generational or culture norms, as well as an individual's weak listening skills and behavioral patterns. Accordingly, to minimize future episodes, I believe that these Five Techniques will help to improve your natural ability to advance your Listening Skills.

1: Face the speaker and keep eye contact.

In most Western cultures, eye contact is considered a common expectation in effective communication. When engaged in a conversation, on a norm, it is expected it that individuals will look each other in the eye. This approach shows courtesy and reassures the person that they have your attention. The challenge is to continue look in their direction, even if they are not reciprocal. Why they not looking directly at you could be due to their development. It is factual that different people display shyness, uncertainty, shame, guilt, or other emotions, along with cultural taboos. Cultural norms, on principles that inhibits eye contact with people under various circumstances.

2: Display attentive and a relaxed posture.

The aim is to appear tentative and comfortable while the person is speaking. That is with a posture that helps to reassure the speaker that they have your attention, as evidence by an occasional intermittent eye contact that confirms your interest to their conversation. Something more attentiveness will reduce the sense of bias or a sense of being judgmental because of the person's race, accents and sex start the process of developing your self-awareness inherit beliefs. In addition, process your self-awareness of any earlier personal bias and misconceptions about other individuals.

3: Keep an open mind.

Keeping an open mind is vital to the art of effective listening due to you have already developed your self-awareness of any inherit beliefs. Now, the best skill is to augment your openness for Critical Thinking. Critical Thinking is to help to display our curiosity thirst for relevance that based on research that we named for biases. Additionally, keeping an open mind strengthen our readiness to process information, as evidence by, an openness to receive another person's opinion and analyze their perspective, without jumping to any conclusions.

4: Listen to the words and try to picture what the speaker is saying.

This is an incredibly challenging a creative phase, I need you to allow your mind to create a mental model of the information being communicated to you. Interpret what the person is saying based on the actual meaning of the words. If have you thought start the drift force yourself to be focus.

5: Avoid interrupting and reframe from interjecting your opinion.

On a norm, we all have been taught that it is rude to interrupt. Therefore, think about the prior four techniques. Face the speaker and keep eye contact. Display attentive and a relaxed posture. Keep an open mind and listen to the words and try to picture what the speaker is say.

In short, the Art of Effective Listening is a continuous process because as humans we are not constant. Each new day, as human we have an array of thoughts, feelings and concerns that consistently demands our attention. Therefore, to display effective listening skills will require our consciousness. Consciously, we must implement healthy listening skills in the early morning to hear what our significant other, children, while driving and as soon as we arrive at work. Consequently, it imperative that we develop a healthy pattern to achieve an Effective Listening Skills. To help advance our communication with others.

11

POSTPARTUM DEPRESSION

Postpartum Depression occurs after childbirth:

personally witness the traumatic effects of my wife, Postpartum Depression. It occurred soon after the birth of our first child, in 1971. On my first visit after the baby's birth, at the hospital. I quickly noticed a mark change in my wife's demeanor. Several days later and once home from the hospital, she continues to show symptoms of the Postpartum Depression. At that time, I had no knowledge of Postpartum Depression or information about a person's psychological needs. Therefore, I just did my best not to annoy her and instead focused on the Baby.

Now, I am aware and educated in the Mental Health practice. I now can clearly recognize that in 1971, my wife, had symptoms of the Postpartum Depression, after the birth of Cassandra. On a norm, both of us are inwardly shy, quiet, and rarely would share internalized emotional thoughts, feelings, and concerns. Therefore, neither of us shared internalized emotions.

In thinking back to 1971, at the time, I also had extreme Mental Health issues. That was evidenced by an array of years of unprocessed Mental and Physical Health concerns. Furthermore, due to my dysfunctional childhood and adolescence developmental years, it is utterly likely, at the time, I had serious undiagnosed Anger Management and other mental health concerns, as evidenced by my poor decision-making concerns.

Since being in the profession, I can now understand the seriousness of Postpartum Depression and the cluster of other Depressions. That could range from mood swings to thoughts of hopelessness, the lack of concentration, insomnia, and ruminated thoughts about fear of the unknown or childbirth pain.

For most women, having a baby is an exciting, joyous occasion, and many anxious moments. But for women with peripartum (formerly postpartum) depression can become very distressing. Peripartum depression refers to depression occurring during pregnancy or after childbirth. The use of the term peripartum recognizes that depression associated with having a baby often begins during pregnancy.

Peripartum depression is a serious, but treatable medical illness involving feelings of extreme sadness, indifference and/or anxiety, as well as changes in energy, sleep, and appetite. It carries risks for the mother and child.

It is estimated **one in seven women experiences peripartum depression**. Pregnancy and the period after delivery can be a particularly vulnerable time for women. Mothers often experience immense biological, emotional, financial, and social changes during this time. There are women that can be at an increased risk for developing mental health problems, particularly depression and anxiety.

Up to 70 percent of all new mothers experience the "baby blues," a short-lasting condition that does not interfere with daily activities and does not require medical attention. Symptoms of this emotional condition may include crying for no reason, irritability, restlessness, and anxiety. These symptoms last a week or two and resolve on their own without treatment.

The purpose of sharing this life experience is to increase awareness about this illness for the significant other in the relationship. In addition, I hope from reading this Chapter that it would encourage the reader to reflect on their mental and physical health status. Additionally, if there are concerns, make the investment for yourself by scheduling an appointment to share them with your Primary Doctor and if needed schedule that first Mental Health Assessment.

12

THE FATHER FIGURE NEED TO DO SPONTANEOUS CHECK-IN WITH CHILDREN

Spontaneous Check-In Opportunities

INTUITION:

I am petitioning that we pledge to evolve and cherish the inherited gift of intuition, regarding our children's well-being. The pledge is to instigate effective "Check-In" opportunities that encourage two-way listening and communication sessions that support in the validation of their "**present state of mind**." Moreover, during those opportune spontaneous "Check-Ins," there should always be one primary Goal. That is to bolster their awareness about your foundational love and support for their wholeness.

The following are nineteen written quotes about Intuition:

> "I believe in intuitions and inspirations...I sometimes feel that I am right. I do not KNOW that I am." — **Albert Einstein**

> "Our bodies have five senses: touch, smell, taste, sight, and hearing. But not to be overlooked are the senses of our souls: intuition, peace, foresight, trust, empathy. The differences between people lie in their use of these senses; most people don't know

anything about the inner senses while a few people rely on them just as they rely on their physical senses, and in fact probably even more." — **C. JoyBell C.**

"Don't try to comprehend with your mind. Your minds are extremely limited. Use your intuition." — **Madeleine L'Engle, <u>A Wind in the Door</u>**

"Intuition is always right in at least two important ways; It is always in response to something. it always has your best interest at heart" — **Gavin De Becker, <u>The Gift of Fear: Survival Signals That Protect Us from Violence</u>**

"Come from the heart, the sincere heart, not the head. When in doubt, choose the heart. This does not mean to deny your own experiences and that which you have empirically learned through the years. It means to trust yourself to integrate intuition and experience. There is a balance, a harmony to be nurtured, between the head and the heart. When the intuition rings clear and true, loving impulses are favored." — **Brian Weiss, <u>Messages from the Masters: Tapping into the Power of Love</u>**

"At times you have to leave the city of your comfort and go into the wilderness of your intuition. What you will discover will be wonderful. What you'll discover is yourself." — **Alan Alda**

"Practice listening to your intuition, your inner voice; ask questions; be curious; see what you see; hear what you hear; and then act upon what you know to be true. These intuitive powers were given to your soul at birth." — **Clarissa Pinkola Estés, Women Who Run with the Wolves: Myths and Stories of the Wild Woman Archetype**

"Emotion often outwits intelligence, while intuition renders life surprisingly fluent and enjoyable. — **Erik Pevernagie**

"When the rusty shackles of our emotions are being unchained, we can become lovers without a cause, and intrinsically the deepest wells of our unconsciousness may uncover the uncharted territories of deliverance, granting free rein to our intuition and giving love downright carte blanche. ("Another empty room")" — **Erik Pevernagie**

"Not too long-ago thousands spent their lives as recluses to find spiritual vision in the solitude of nature. Modern man need not become a hermit to achieve this goal, for it is neither ecstasy nor world-estranged mysticism his era demands, but a balance between quantitative and qualitative reality. Modern man, with his reduced ability for intuitive belief, is unlikely to receive help from the contemplative life of a hermit in the wilderness. But what he can do is to give undivided attention, at times, to a natural phenomenon, seeing it in detail, and recalling all the scientific facts about it he may remember. Gradually, however, he must silence his thoughts and, for moments at least, forget all his personal cares and desires, until nothing still is in his soul but awe for the miracle before him. Such efforts are like journeys beyond the boundaries of narrow self-love and, although the process of intuitive awakening is laborious and slow, its rewards are noticeable from the very first. If pursued through the course of years, something will begin to stir in the human soul, a sense of kinship with the forces of life consciousness which rule the world of plants and animals, and with the powers which figure out the laws of matter. While analytical intellect may well be called the most precious fruit of the Modern Age, it must not be allowed to rule supreme in matters of cognition. If science is to bring happiness and real progress to the world, it needs the warmth of man's heart just as much as the cold inquisitiveness of his brain." — **Franz Winkler**

"The truth about life and lie about life is not measured by others but by your intuition, which never lies." — **Santosh Kalwar**

"Intuition is a sense of knowing how to act spontaneously, without needing to know why." — **Sylvia Clare, <u>Trusting Your Intuition: Rediscover Your True Self to Achieve a Richer, More Rewarding Life</u>**

"Being spontaneous is being able to respond with confidence; calmly trusting that, whatever the outcome, you will have a positive if challenging experience that will lead to greater self-awareness and success." — **Sylvia Clare, <u>Trusting Your Intuition: Rediscover Your True Self to Achieve a Richer, More Rewarding Life</u>**

"Faith requires following the power of a whisper."
— **Shannon L. Alder**

"Meditation is an essential travel partner on your journey of personal transformation. Meditation connects you with your soul, and this connection gives you access to your intuition, your heartfelt desires, your integrity, and the inspiration to create a life you love." — **Sarah McLean**

"To know how to choose a path with heart is to learn how to follow intuitive feeling. Logic can tell you superficially where a path might lead to, but it cannot judge whether your heart will be in it."
— **Jean Shinoda Bolen**

"The Islamic intellectual tradition has usually not seen a dichotomy between intellect and intuition but has created a hierarchy of knowledge and methods of attaining knowledge according to which degrees of both intellection and intuition become harmonized in an order encompassing all the means available to man to know, from sensual knowledge an reason to intellection and inner version or the "knowledge of the heart." — **Seyyed Hossein Nasr, Islamic Philosophy from Its Origin to the Present: Philosophy in the Land of Prophecy**

"What good is intuition if your heart gets in the way of hearing it?" — **Shannon Alder**

"Intuition comes in several forms:
-    a sudden flash of insight, visual or auditory

- a predictive dream
- a spinal shiver of recognition as something is occurring or told to you
- a sense of knowing something already
- a sense of having already experienced something actually being
- a snapshot image of a future scene or event
- knowledge, perspective or understanding divined from tools which respond to the subconscious mind"

— **Sylvia Clare, Trusting Your Intuition: Rediscover Your True Self to Achieve a Richer, More Rewarding Life**

"We all have an inner voice, our personal whisper from the universe. All we must do is listen -- feel and sense it with an open heart. Sometimes it whispers of intuition or precognition. Other times, it whispers an awareness, a remembrance from another plane. Dare to listen. Dare to hear with your heart." — **CJ Heck, Bits and Pieces: Short Stories from a Writer's Soul**

"There is no such thing as chance. Everything occurs because of cause and effect; what you do now will create your own future."

"Intuition means exactly what it sounds like, in-tuition! An inner tutor or teaching and learning mechanism that takes us forward daily. It is a resource that, where recognized, has infinite potential." — **Sylvia Clare, Trusting Your Intuition: Rediscover Your True Self to Achieve a Richer, More Rewarding Life**

"Success is realizing the true joy and wonder of life can only be yours if you follow your own intuition, aiming to achieve your bliss." — **Steven Redhead, The Solution**

"Life is really remarkably simple. In each moment, we could choose between saying "yes" or "no," to listen to our intuition, to listen to our true inner voice, the Existential voice within ourselves. When we say "yes," we have contact with Existence and we receive nourishment, love, joy, support, and inspiration. When we say "no," we create a separation from life and begin to create dreams and expectations of how it should be. We begin to live in the memories of the past and in the fantasies of the future – as if any other time than here and now really could make us happy and satisfied." — **Swami Dhyan Giten, Presence - Working from Within. The Psychology of Being**

"Intuition is the art of the moment. Intuition is always in the moment, in the here and now. While the intellect always moves like the pendulum of a clock between the memories of the past and the fantasies of the future, intuition is always in the moment, always in the here and now. The more we develop our inner being, the inner source of love and truth, the inner quality of being here and now, the more we also have access to our intuition." — **Swami Dhyan Giten, Presence - Working from Within. The Psychology of Being**

In closing, I genuinely believe that the pain and heartbreak that comes from losing a child, is one of the most everlasting saddest in a Father Figure's lifetime. Therefore, as ***One Body in Christ***, together we will pledge to recognize and used our God's giving gift of Intuition, as showed by, instigating "Spontaneous Check-In" with all our children.

13

ONE-ON-ONE MEETINGS WITH CHILDREN MEMBERS

Once a month or weekly or randomly schedule a one-on-one Meetings with each of your children. The aim is to repeatedly teach them that they are the future, and that your Long-Term Role is to help them to evolve into the Adult Phase of Life.

In this Chapter I will encourage one-on-one Parent and Child engagements. The foundation of the meetings will be based on discussions about their children's unique individuality. In addition, parents will practice the art of strengthen their children's awareness about their individuality. Also, the parent explains to the child the long- and short-term reasons for the establishment of having consistent pattern of one-on-one meetings, within the home and, if needed, those children that are living outside of an immediate parent's home.

One ideal Short-Term Goal is to reassure children about their uniqueness. The child may not be the tallest or smartest person in the classroom; yet all are gifted due to the glory of the Lord. An example of a Second Goal could be about ways to discuss why they should cherish their uniqueness in a positive manner that emulate the body of self-pride. The Third example is to encourage them to use the meetings as an opportunity to freely have an open two-way communication about their thoughts, feelings, and concerns, as well as opinions. There is never a limit on what up for discussion during on-on-one meeting, due to the agreement that once the meeting mutually ends, all discussions, attitudes, passions, and disagreements will need to be place on hold, until the next schedule meeting. This is a major specifically important agreement regarding the one-on-one discussions.

The one-on-one approach in the short term will have an everlasting impression through-out the child's life if it is correctly applied. At times, there may be occasions for brief meetings and likewise, there will be extendedly long one-on-one meetings. The usefulness of both types of meetings are that you are teaching them how to start the process of having a healthy debate. All meetings will need to address the child's prevailing concerns and need, as well as internalized emotion, in a safe and non-judgmental environment. The key is to be honest with your words and commitments. If the topic is a challenging and you need time to think and to do some research on the topic, table the discussion. With a promise to review at the next meeting.

The long-term value of these meetings is a child's reflection of their parent taking the time to stop and attend one-on-one meetings with them to listen to their thoughts, feelings, and concerns, in a non-judgmental manner. The desired outcome is enormous for our children's reassurance that they are special to their parent.

This is vital in a family because both parties are being respectful in learning the hard reality about each other's thoughts, suggestions, and beliefs that are the foundation of their individual's opinion. This approach will help to enhance the valuable of effective two-way communication, without having any exhibited unregulated emotions. Likewise, encourages our children to start the process of processing the concept of having a healthy debate and the challenges of having a one-on-one meeting where each person displays an effective listening and communication skills.

Therefore, Father Figures need to encourage one-on-one two-way communications that allows formal discussion on any topic, in which opposing arguments are discussed in a professional disposition. Why, because this approach helps to develop our children's openness to another's person's communication.

Without having embedded challenging three words **"But I'm Right."** It took me over fifty years to finally understanding being "Right" will not always gain you favor. Therefore, I am suggesting in this chapter that Father Figures instruct children and adolescence healthy ways to debate their ideas. In addition, learn how to recognize if the other party is even listening to what you are saying.

Once again, the Father Figures will need to schedule one-on-one meetings with the children and adolescences during their developmental years. The topic of the meeting will vary. One-on-one Meeting is an opportune moment to start the process of developing our children's Debate Skills. Another is to convince them, **beyond any shadow of a doubt**, that they are incredibly special individuals and that they must always love themselves. Furthermore, seek inventive ways to address anything that troubles them during the scheduled one-on-one Meetings. Additionally, remind them about the Family's Time-Out, choice. Next, reassure them of their awareness about your love for them. Lastly, take the time to repeatedly teach them that they are the future, and that your Long-Term Role is to help them to evolve into the Adult Stages of Life.

14

THE NEED TO SCHEDULE PROFESSIONAL THERAPY SESSIONS

Professional Therapy

The primary aims of Professional Therapy are to develop the Participant /Individual, or Family, or Couple, or Group's awareness about how to implement healthier coping skills. Towards the Goals to better manage Anger, Disappointments, Stress, and a host of other causes of unregulated emotions, thoughts, feelings, and concerns. In short, Professional Therapy is helping to develop growth and understand about mental health concerns, root causes and how to implement the pathway for recovery.

It estimated that 40% of Americans are actively engaged in Professional Therapy or other form of psychotherapy. Consequently, what's even better is the report that 36% of Americans are open to Professional Therapy. Hence, the stigma label about Therapy, appears to have diminished and is no longer parallel with shame or disgrace. The hope is for more people to be open to the urgency of Professional Therapy as an efficient approach to better manage unregulated emotions, thoughts, feelings, and concerns.

The best result from having Therapy is that the Participant consistently appraise obstacles that are hindering their willingness to adopt "The Five Stages of change." That are Precontemplation, Contemplation, Preparation, Action, and Maintenance, as well as the Terminations Stage of change.

Precontemplation is the stage at which there is no intention or self-awareness of a need to change their behavior. The major problem is that Participants that are in this stage are unaware or under-aware of their problems.

Contemplation is the stage in which a participant is aware that a personal problem, within them, exists and is seriously thinking about overcoming it but have not yet made a commitment to take any actions.

Preparation is the stage that combines intention and the behavioral criteria. The participant at this stage is intending to act in the next month; however, they have unsuccessfully acted in the past year.

Action is the stage in which a participant changes their behavior, experiences, or environment to address their problems. Action involves the most overt behavioral changes and requires considerable commitment of time and energy.

Maintenance is the hardest stage because it is the stage in which a participant struggles every minute of the day. To prevent another relapse episode that exhibited unregulated emotions or showed unhealthy behavior patterns. Moreover, the goals are to vindicate their commitment to the continuation and consolidation from the Action Stage of change. For a participant with an history of having mental health concerns, this stage extends from six months to an undetermined period past the first Action Stage of Change. In other words, it is the Maintenance Stage that they would need to repeat each day, hour, minute, second, and micro-second for the rest of the participant's life.

Termination Stage, participants have zero enticement and are certain that they will not relapse to a prior undesirable propensity as a method for adapting or responding to the challenge of a disparaging social interaction.

Once the participant, or couple, embrace these Five Stages of Change, that shown by their established healthier behavioral patterns and social interactions. Then this will "**set-the-stage**" for the Participant to emulate the fruit of **Forgiveness and Unconditional Love**.

Pros of Therapy

One of the pros for Therapy, is that it provides you with a State License Professional Therapist to talk with. On a norm, it is hard for people to share personnel emotion, especially with a stranger, like a therapist. In general, people get anxiety and do not feel comfortable sharing their shameful secrets to a stranger.

Also, Therapy aids in learning the values of having a healthy debate on an array of topics. Learning to debate promotes our listening, presentation, and communication skills. Additionally, one of the aims of Therapy is to rationally look in the mirror at yourselves. Then for the first time in their life, which helps to set stage for constructive criticism, for two main reasons. One is, learning how to appreciate the gift in processing a clinical opinion about the Participant's exhibited presentation. The second is, to recognize the factual reality regarding mental health concerns, as evidenced by their history of exhibited presentation and unhealthy decision-making skills. Therapist challenge is to increase the participant's self-awareness about clinical techniques to help them better process diagnosed mental health concerns and other unhealthy social interaction presentations.

The most common type of therapy is Psychotherapy, which is based on personal interaction with a person to change behavior and overcome problematic behavioral patterns. There are pros for learning how to start this process. One is learning to implement effective coping skills to better manage and improve their decision-making skills.

Therapy starts with the participant having a Biopsychosocial Assessment to make a clinical assessment of their mental health diagnosis. Next, phase is for the Therapist and participant to work together in the development of their 30-Day Treatment Plan. The Treatment Plan is to start the process of addressing the identified mental health concerns. The next phase is to mutually develop the participant's 90 Days Treatment Plan. The updated Plan is to address concerns and discover triggers that are at the root cause of the participant's mental health concerns.

This therapeutic approach will help in psychoanalyzing the participant's mental health status. Moreover, therapist support the participant's clinical process in implementing productive coping mechanisms to reduce and better manage future unhealthy episodes.

In addition, being actively engaged in therapy will help the participant to better understand their underlying mental health and unhealthy development years life experiences. In reference to learning, therapy help in focusing on the development of efficient coping skills that will help them in addressing embedded developmental years unhealthy presentations. Furthermore, therapy provides a participant with the opportunity to experience the therapeutic welcoming atmosphere of being in safe environment. Then the participant starts to develop serene feelings **that makes them ready to trust**. This is the initial stage where Participant and Therapist, rapport is being strengthen. As their rapport is strengthen, therapy is complimented and the establishment of their Genuine Trust. Trust between the Therapist and Participant is a requirement.

Finally, while in Treatment and after the development of the 90 Days Treatment Plan. The future Treatment Plans will need to continue to project the participant's future Goals and Objectives. As well as, challenging them to work on the Five Stages of Change. Then the next phase is the Maintenance Stage and writing down their Yearly or Two-Years, and other future Goals and Objectives.

Cons of Therapy

One of the foremost downsides of being in therapy is finding the ideal counselling program and Counselor. This task can be exhausting because of the reality of finding that ideal fit – happy medium for that healthy social interaction between Counselors, are challenging. That is based on the participant's anxiety in combination with a sense of vulnerability. On a norm participant will often display minimum engagement with the Counselor until there is a level of rapport, between the Therapist and Participant.

The early stage of the vulnerability period can lead to transference. The common psychotherapeutic term, meaning the transference of certain feelings or emotions to their therapist.

These are the three types of transference: Positive, Negative and Sexualized.

The sexualized type is when the participant may develop

romantic feelings for the therapist, which can negatively affect the participant-therapist relationship.

The negative transference means there is an antagonistic environment during the therapy that is blocking the achievement of a therapeutic situation.

If either of Sexualized or Negative type of transference happen. The participant should seek out a different Therapist. I would strongly recommend that the participant do not give-up because most times, finding the precise Counselor is the hardest task.

The Positive Transference: Is once there is an appearance of an unadulterated participant and therapist rapport. It is then, that the therapeutic process begins.

Additionally, one common concern that may occur after the two to three consistent weeks of attending therapy is participant avoidance. The participant starts to avoid prior common social interactions with friends, and family members. This type of self-isolation is counterproductive towards the participant's long-term goal. To address this concern, Therapist will support the participant in understanding how sharing internalized emotions with family members and healthy social interrelationships will help to strengthen engagement.

The other concern with Therapy is a participant's pattern of rotating from In-patient to Out-patient. Because their transition from Inpatient to Outpatient, will cause some level of emotional instability. Instability that could hinder their long-term personal mental health journey, as shown by their consistent commitment to address needed behavioral changes, in an outpatient arrangement.

15

THE ACTIVE ENGAGEMENT
IN COUNSELING

The Active Engagement in Counselling

Diagnosis: The Assessment

The start of Counselling, with a License Professional or Social Worker, starts with getting Biopsychosocial Assessment. Which systematically consider biological, psychological, and social factors and their complex interactions in understanding the participant's health. The root causes of any diagnose can be array from developmental dysfunctional thinking and unprocessed anxiety, as well as the participant's needs for medications. Medications to address their history of depression and trauma. In addition, to Treatment Criteria for Addictive, Substance-Related and Co-Occurring Conditions.

Understanding:

The participants who are experiencing mental health issues do not even realize that they are having problems. Besides, participants that do realize that something is wrong, they are often confused as to why they are having unregulated erratic behavioral patterns or unhealthy decision-making episodes.

I remember the first time, while in Couple Therapy, that the Therapist told me that "yelling at my wife was an act of verbal abuse and it was more offensive than hitting a woman." To my shock and lack of understand of how yelling is more offensive than hitting a woman. Just thinking about doing something that was more offensive than hitting a woman, made me feel very ashamed of myself. Therefore, I immediately stopped yelling at my wife or anyone and started the process of processing my serious need for Anger Management, as well as redirected my spare time towards doing something productive. Therefore, I enrolled in Regis University's MBA Program.

Moreover, to reflect on the hard facts that it took me more than fifty-five years of my life to finally "**Understand**" that yelling at anyone is an exhibited **Offensive Behavior Pattern.** This is another reason I decided to author this book.

My hope is that Individuals, Families and Couples start the practice of investing Therapy. Especially, during their early adolescence (ages 11 to 14 years old); middle adolescence (ages 15 to 17 years old; late adolescence, ages 18 to 21 years old); or early adult stages of their life. The truth is that each of us have symptoms of mental health concerns. I am asking you to have a Biopsychosocial Assessment and then review the results with the Therapist of your choice.

16

SUBSTANCE ABUSE COUNSELING

The Important of Substance Abuse Counselling

Most addictions are more than a physical dependence on a particular substance. Therefore, even after a participant have detoxed and their physical reliance is at a very manageable level. The risk of relapsing is still high. Oftentimes, the participant's psychological and social battles against their addiction are more overpowering than their physical battles. During the detoxifying or even after doing so, the participant will experience the following: A combination of stress and anxiety that linked to their change in lifestyle, habits, and in their diet. Furthermore, there is the environment factors from the participant's prior triggers. From the smell of smoke, a whiff of alcohol, or even an advertisement of an item that connects them to their prior addicted behavioral patterns.

The participant reoccurring struggles from ruminations of dysfunctional social interactions network of like-minded substance individuals. That entails family members, friends from school, Addiction Programs, and many other dark places. Other, stressful circumstance are the incidental family members and friends that go out of their way to invite the participant (who is in recovery), to go with them as support, while they purchase alcohol, cocaine, oxycodone, and a variety of an abusive substance to achieve euphoria. These factors are the breadcrumbs that could lead to another relapse episode.

This is when the Professional Addiction Counselor will exemplify rational clinical techniques to support the participant in the mutual development of their Treatment Plan. It is the Treatment Plan's Goals and Objectives that guides the participant's pathway to recovery. As they mutually discuss how to best address the participant's Treatment Plan Goals and Objectives.

Four Addiction Counselling Methodology

These four different Addiction Counseling Methodologies are widespread. They are Individual, Group, Outpatient, and Residential. I would share that none of them are known to be better than the others. Likewise, there is no single approach for a single type of addiction. The Addiction Counselor is the person to make an assessment for the participant's clinical structure.

Individual Therapy is good for the one-on-one approach to allow the participant time to focus on their mental health concerns. **Group Therapy** is when there are other individuals with similar addictive challenges. This approach encourage participant to share their story. As well as work together to support each other. **Outpatient Treatment** schedules are sympathetic to the participant's work or school requirements, as shown by scheduling treatment either in the morning, afternoon, and evenings. **Residential Treatment** primary goal is to separate the participant from their environment that has caused them to engage in addictive and unhealthy behavioral patterns.

Pros of Substance Abuse Counselling

THE POWER OF POSITIVE THINKING

Through counseling, the power of positive thinking is expected to support the participant in understanding the root causes of their diagnosed **Mental Health Disorder.** That promote the participant's confidence and self-esteem.

See life in a better light

With therapy, the participant goal is to see the status of their life. Then set goals to address needed changes towards a new and unique perspective. Jointly, there are discussions about how much better their life would be when the participant achieves a substance free lifestyle from any addictive behavior. Ideally, the aim is for the participant's attitude towards life will instigate their desire for a more positive perspective.

Affirm your self-worth

Therapy will help the participant recognize the importance of their self-worth. Thus, increasing their awareness about the implantation of healthier approaches to better manage their quality of life and get grounded in the newfound feeling of their autonomy. The participant's thoughts of autonomy will help them to project a renewed sense of hope. Therapist primary task, at this stage is to enhance participant's awareness about the correlation of their addictive lifestyle, as evidence by, repeated relapse episodes. Is grounded in unhealthy thoughts and feelings of helplessness, uselessness, and hopelessness. Contrasted to positive thoughts that reaffirm the participant's self-worth by the implementation of effective therapeutic techniques. Towards the long-term goal implementing effective skills to better manage recovery.

Help you make better life decisions

During the episodes of a participant's addiction, there are many examples of poor decision-making skills. The goal to counter-poor decision-making skills are therapeutic weeks of constructive counseling sessions. That address the participant's readiness to implement effective techniques to better manage their decisions making skills. These therapeutic session's objective is to strengthen their ability to better manage an array of issues in a more productive and positive manner.

Cons Of Substance Abuse Counselling

Could be Long Methodical Process

Addiction counseling and the combination of therapeutic participant/counselor relationship takes time because of the methodical process. Therefore, Counselor and Participant must embrace the art of patience. The patience in addressing the stages of change and implementation of clinical techniques to better manage their unique Long-Term Recovery.

Costly

The Addiction Counseling process can be expensive, and a percentage could be outside the guideline of the Insurance Plan. While the participant is engaged in the Substance Abuse Counseling. The facts that there are variations of how long a participant will need to be in a Substance Abuse Recovery Program and the unknown will create a level of stress for the participant.

Logically, it is great to use money for self-development; however, due to the participant's addictive behavior pattern. The likelihood of having discretionary money is not likely. If there is discretionary money or mental insurance to cover the expense, we all would agree, this is the time for the participant to invest in their Long-Term Recovery. If there is extra income or medical insurance, this is the time that the participant should seriously invest in themselves. As an approach to strengthen their coping skills versus leaving too soon and experience another relapse episode.

Backfiring

At times, the participant's pessimistic thinking may lead them to conclude that all their efforts are only resulting into unpleasant and negativity stress since their enrollment in therapy. Participant may falsely believe that the unwelcome news, unhappy events, circumstances are due to being in Therapy. The therapist role is to support the participant in processing, life situations sober, without the comfort of using an addictive substance. Similarly, this is also when the therapist will need to encourage two-way communication and active listening techniques. As Participant and Therapist process the participant's internalized unregulated thoughts, feelings, and concerns. The therapist will acknowledge the participant's anxieties and then therapeutically, support participant in developing skills to better embrace concerns in a healthy therapeutic manner, as well as displaying a non-judgmental presentation.

17

PRO AND CONS OF MARRIAGE COUNSELING

The Pros and Cons of Marriage Counseling

Once couples realize that something is wrong with their **marriage,** there are several choices they can make. They can read Self-help Books or try to fix it themselves or seek advice from friends and a family member, as well as doing nothing. Just hoping that things going to get better is never the solution. Each of these options will have varying results; however, doing nothing have the least chance for success.

Most couples do not have the experience to know how to navigate through tough marital interpersonal concerns, within the home. They fell in love and expected the fairytale life. Then they the reality, he snores, or she snores at night, they no longer treat me the same, he thinks I am a maid because he does not clean-up after themselves, they no longer treat me the same and we argue most of the time. Then there repeat unhealthy thoughts of sadness because of the sudden change in their marriage. It is common for Married Couples to struggle and wonder "why are we having these types of problems." Therefore, the best solution is Marriage Counseling.

A Marriage Counselor primary responsibility is to enhance couple's awareness about the development of effective methods, together as one Team, to resolve conflict within the family and specially within their marriage, as well as social interactions that are outside of the home. As the couple consistently function independent of any third party.

The challenge for the Therapist is to encourage that the couple start by having an open discussion about each of their expectations. Both parties write down their expectations and then actively engage in a respectful two-way healthy conversation. The objective is for both participants to start the process of establishing a mutually agreement regarding each other's expectations.

Also, the Therapist will support couples in learning healthy techniques to find problem areas within their marriage and what is most significant, is developing ways to improve their two-way communication skills and their effective listening skills.

As with anything, marriage counseling has its pros and cons.

Pros of Marriage Counseling

The overall goal of Marriage Counselor is to support couples in finding healthy solutions to resolve issues, improve and strengthen their marriage. Other Therapist's roles are to help married couples uncovers unproductive interacting that has been detrimental to the progress of their marriage.

With the License Professional Counselor supporting both participants, as the neutral third-party manner. Therapist's average Counseling Sessions will involve their clinical observation from seeing the couples share frustrations and interaction towards each other. The Therapist offers methods to better manage disputes, disagreements, and problems when they arise. The use of personality assessments or other techniques to improve their communication style and effective listening skills.

How well couples relate with their counselor is the most extensive component in any Therapeutic Session. Both Spouses should treat the choice of researching for a Marriage Therapist like a job interview. With the understanding that each will equally need to feel that proficient sense of genuine rapport and comfort with the selected Professional Counselor. Moreover, throughout the therapeutic progress, **couples must not be afraid to stop, pause or if needed to once again resume researching for a different Therapist. If either or both couples suddenly develop a sense of disconnect with the Marriage Professional.**

CONS

Marriage counseling does not always work for everyone, and at times will uncover issues that are unsolvable. Two of the major roadblocks are one or both couples' resistance towards the concept of Forgiveness and Unconditional Love.

Another concern, is the encounter where one or both spouses are totally resistance to the Five Stage of Change, as evidenced by their lack of willingness to inwardly recognize their exhibited unhealthy behavior patterns and readiness to start the Five Stages of Change. It is important to remember: One spouse cannot fix a broken marriage; it takes both spouses to dedicate their commitment to discuss what changes are they willing to make. Or, to respectful clearly explain and listen to each other's thoughts, feelings, and concerns.

A common task for each couple is that each one would write out what are their current concerns and desired expectations. Furthermore, both partners are **obligated to take responsibility** for their role in the problems. The widespread problem with this approach is an Individual readiness to take responsibility and to recognize that they have mental health concerns, as evidenced by their frequent exhibited unhealthy decision-making skills or dysfunctional social interactions that is also amplified by their history of several Anger Management presentations.

In addition, Marriage Counseling is normally not a quick fix. It will take over on average 12 to 24 Counseling Sessions, dependent on the seriousness of the discrepancies. This presents an economical expense on the family. Too often, married couples cannot afford the cost of an ongoing therapy more than three or five Sessions. Once the discretionary money is gone and other household bills are paramount. Eventually the spouses will drop out or try to fix their problems themselves. Please note: Help may still be available through local Marriage Support Groups or at places of Worship which may offer Marriage Counseling free or at a significantly lesser expense than a Professional Therapist.

Taking the first step to participate in Marriage Counseling is always the hardest one. The challenge is that on a norm people do not receive change with enthusiasm. The approach to address change is a slow dance. That will need the participant to have an open mind and dedication to try their best to work on the concerns within the marriage.

Marriage is based on **Forgiveness and Unconditional Love**. In a productive and healthy manner that helps to fortify the family's belief of togetherness, as One Body in Christ.

18

PROS AND CONS OF GROUP THERAPY VS INDIVIDUAL THERAPY

Weighing the Pros and Cons of Group Therapy vs Individual Therapy

Ambika Taylor April 24, 2021, News Comments Off on Weighing the Pros and Cons of Group Therapy vs Individual Therapy 140 Views

Almost twenty percent of Americans report attending a form of therapy in 2019. If therapy is something you are considering, it is important to look at the appointment options. The two most common are individual and group sessions.

Group therapy involves attending a therapy session run by a professional counselor with multiple participants. Group therapy is not as popular as individual therapy, but there are benefits that those in individual therapy will not receive.

Individual therapy is the practice of a singular person receiving personalized treatment from a professional. Despite being the most popular treatment method, individual therapy has its downsides.

When comparing group therapy vs individual therapy, it is important to look at the benefits and disadvantages of both.

19

FAMILY THERAPY

Why Family Therapy?

Families can find themselves in the middle of very tough situations. This includes divorce, an upcoming second marriage, addiction problems within the Family, or even having to deal with a death in the family member. Family Therapy can be of help in getting a Family through a crisis and in many other circumstances.

Why is coming together as a Family for Counseling an effective method? These are seven reasons:

- Family Members can learn effective and healthier ways to communicate with each other.
- Family Members can resolve all types of issues related to siblings.
- Family Members can define and understand their specific roles in the family unit.
- Family Members can learn his or her strengths and weaknesses.
- Family Members can learn effective ways to resolve concerning issues.
- Family Members can discover ways that parents and children can communicate better.
- Family Members can discuss various challenges that are currently experiencing.

Situations that involve addiction or the sudden death of a loved one can inflict havoc within any peaceful Family. Due to the challenge of how each family member process and resolve information. In reference to Grief and Loss. Family Counseling set the format for an environment of equality. Where all family members have equal rights, liberties, and status to the freedom of expressing their thoughts, feelings, and concerns. That evidence by the Family Therapy's guidelines to reduce tension, stress, and help to start the process of processing internalized emotions.

Why Therapy: For over fifty years, I was in denial of having any mental health concerns. The real question is how I could not have several diagnosed Mental Health Disorders. Because, as an African American growing up in an environment of prejudice, discrimination, being marginalized because of my racial or ethnic group. Plus, to daily witness individual and cultural racism, as well as attitudes of superiority due to institutional racism. Unknown to me about how the persistent exposure of oppression has caused me to experience traumatic episodes of psychological trauma. In combination, with my many years of unprocessed Baggage from my developmental years.

Why Therapy: I lived with Mental Health concerns of many traumatic episodes and the adverse effect from my developmental years, as well as supported the concept of the generational curse. The doctrine that individuals inherit the judgement for the sin of their ancestor. The developmental period where children seriously need exposure to the Nurtured Heart of Forgiveness, Unconditional Love and The Father Figure Commitment within a healthy home environment.

Why Therapy: What troubles me the most is how I lived with unprocessed mental health concerns, for over fifty years, and never had any thought to make an appointment with a License Mental Health Provider.

CONCLUSION

In thinking about all the people throughout the world that died for COVID-19, just in the years 2019 to 2021. As of November 17, 2021, the number was 4,547,782 according to the World Health Organization. In another scenario, reflect on Childhood births deformity and deformities that are congenital: present at birth, developmental; appearing later in their childhood; gotten because it caused an injuries or illnesses.

In addition, I will share with you something I would repetitively witness that happen to me, when I drove to hospital in Roosevelt Island, Queens, New York, to see my mother. On my once-a-month trip, I always found myself stressing about an array of concerns like bills, racism within the workplace or communities, and a host of other situations.

Until I arrived on the floor where my mother was located. It always seemed that with each step closer and closer to her, the smile on her face would get larger and larger. Finally, when I am at her bedside, my mother would be expressing her happiness by her noticeably big smile. Still today, my thoughts from at moment, still today; makes me cry. As I reflect, just thinking about that precious moment in my life.

The first topic my mother would speak about is, "I have no more pain." I thought to myself, is that she no longer in pain is because my oldest brother Tommy signed for the operation that my father refused to sign. The surgery was to stop my mother pain by operating on her Spinal Cord. The outcome resulted in no pain and my mother's body features were never the same.

I would acknowledge her happiness of not having any more pain and start conversations about my mother's sisters and brothers, about my four brothers and best of all, with a sparkle of excitement in her eyes, we would always talk about what was going on with her husband, my father.

When ending my visit and slowly walking towards the exit door, I would look back at her, for another life moment to connect with my mother's smile.

In returning to my car, I exhale to picture my mother's smile, again. Then after about 5 minutes, I start the trip back home. I would once again, discover that I really do not have any serious problems. How clear it is to why I am extremely fortunate. As an alternative, to me thinking that I was driving to cheer my mother up; however, each time, I would discover how she would always flip the script. My mother would instead cheer me up. The experience of being in her presence would bring me back to the reality and the overall scheme of things on how my problems are not really problems at all.

So, I would like you to take away from reading this book are the importance of always showing Unconditional Love and Forgiveness, towards your family members, peers, and people within your community, as well as your circle of friends. I would expect you to develop the habit of always role modeling the Holy Spirit of Unconditional Love and Forgiveness.

Also, I hope that this book strengthens millions of Father's Figures commitment to consistent emulate their Role-Model within the Family and Mental Health awareness about themselves and others. Furthermore, the aim is to encourage people to focus on how blessed they are, just by awaken-up with a sound mind and body. Time is better focused on healthy ways to nurture Family members, social interactions, and individuals within the community.

In thinking "I am Ok" and that there is nothing mentally or physically wrong, with me. However, at the time, I am oblivious to the importance of my Father Figure Commitment, role.

Therefore, I failed in the maintenance of a fortified home environment that encourages both parents and children to work together in practicing the Nurtured Heart, Forgiveness and Unconditional Love presentation within and outside of the Home.

What troubles me the most is how I lived with unprocessed mental health concerns. Mental health concerns that could have had an adverse effect on my children's early developmental years. A behavior that supported the concept of the generational curse. The doctrine that individuals inherit the judgement for the sin of their ancestor. The developmental period where children seriously need exposure to the Nurtured Heart of Forgiveness, Unconditional Love and The Father Figure Commitment within a healthy home environment.

I am suggesting that anytime the Holy Spirit within you makes you feel or sense someone's detrimental intent, then pray. Pray for them and leave it in God's unchanging Hands.

So, in closing, I would like to reiterate why you will need to pause once you to realize that you are angry. From the moment of your unregulated emotions, it is very highly likely for you to make an irrational decision.

I have learned that if I am having a discussion with someone or group of people and I start to get a stomachache or headache or the combination of both. I now know that it is time for me to remove myself from this conversation or situation. It took me over fifty-five years to learn, why it is vital that I need to break away and if that not possible, I need to stop talking and do my best to avoid making any comment or statement. As evidenced by history of my argumentative and serious disagreements that resulted in me making irresponsible comments or statements while I was angry. The bottom line, I never once made a good decision while being Angry.

Now, I take immense pride in consistently emulating the Holy Spirit of Unconditional Love and the heart of Forgiveness, as a rational healthy Christian.

The importance of Unlimited Forgiveness. New Living Translation

> MATTHEW 18:21. *Then Peter came to HIM and asked, Lord, how often shall I forgive someone who sin against me? Seven times?*

> MATTHEW 18:22. *"No, not seven times," Jesus replied, "but seventy times seven."*

THE END

ACKNOWLEDGMENTS

I would like to acknowledge the following people. Theresa Brown, Cassandra Brown, Octavia Brown, Jennifer Brown and Crystal Smith as well as Philadelphia Biblical University, PBU.

To Theresa Brown, the mother of my only three children. I apologize, to you, for all the lost years due to my inconsistent exhibited Father Figure Role Model and spiritual immaturity within our Marriage. The root cause of our Divorce was clearly due to my lack of forgiveness, unconditional love, and my inability to emulate the Father Figure Commitment role throughout our Marriage.

Theresa and I, first met in the Summer of 1969. Both had recently turned 18 years old. On October 10, 1970, we married at a Church on Gun Hill Road area in the Bronx, New York. Within the first month of our marriage, we had moved into an apartment on Mickle Ave in the Bronx that was across the street from Theresa Grandparents, Parents, 3 Sisters and 2 Brothers.

Prior to our marriage, I started working for New York Telephone Company, New York City, New York, as of February 16, 1970. In 1972, the arrival of our first child, Cassandra, was born on April 5, 1971.

My first serious challenge in being the provider for my immediate family occurred on July 13, 1971. On that date, Joseph A. Beirne, the President of the Communication Workers of America, announced that as of 6AM tomorrow, July 14, 1971, all 500,000 union workers would strike the nation's Telephone System. This strike lasted seven months. Therefore, while on strike I drove for a neighborhood Cab Company part-time, to make extra money. This was my first life experience of having serious Bills and obligations to provide for my new immediate family daily needs.

Household needs for food requirements, transportation and the array of normal expenses that occurs within a family. Besides rent being the biggest expense, the other was an unexpected hospital bill. Theresa's 30 Days of hospitalization during the last month of pregnancy. New York Telephone Company decline coverage because of my lack of service by one month for full coverage.

Therefore, at age of nineteen, I had obligations and limited awareness of my inability to communicate internalized emotions to my wife or everyone else. Instead, I allowed negative emotions to ruminate. These unhealthy emotions encouraged unhealthy decisions making that resulted in a pattern of unhealthy behavior. My unhealthy behavior patterns help set the stage for over fifty-five years of unproductive and unhealthy life experiences. That was due to my lack of awareness about the importance of being a productive role model. Role model that displayed unconditional love, forgiveness, and modeled leadership in an empathic manner.

It was not until I retired from Verizon after thirty-six years of Service, I felt a grave need to learn precise information about the Bible. Therefore, I enrolled in Philadelphia Biblical Foundation Program. After I completed the Program, I decided to seek my master's degree in Christian Counseling and the Certificate of Advanced Specialization in Christian Counseling, between the years of 2006 to 2012.

I feel genuinely blessed to finally have the wisdom to pause and then be directed by the Spirit of The Lord. My obedience has allowed me to achieve a sense of enlightenment about the value of surrendering to His Will. In addition, my obedience has helped me to start the process of self-reflection and most important emulate the Nurtured Heart concept of Forgiveness, unconditional love, and the Father Figure Role Model commitment. Furthermore, I gained a more precise understanding of the sixty-six Stories that are written in the Bible.

The icing on the cake for me was my first trip to Israel. Those two weeks in Israel set the stages for everlasting changes in life forever.

To my three lovely daughters Cassandra, Octavia, and Jennifer Brown. I am sincerely sorry for not consistently showing Unconditional Love as a devoted Father Figure during their early developmental years.

The failures that I displayed help to amplify my inability to Biblical Balance my Father Figure Commitment. Also, to consistently embrace my Family Responsibilities, show healthy social interactions with external family members, display a common pattern of emotional empathy towards all of God's Children. Too often, displayed extremely Poor Decision-Making and, Anger Management Skills, as well as unhealthy behavior patterns. Furthermore, I extremely lacked the value of having an honest and healthy debate, and the glory of learning about another person's Values, Wants/Needs, Decisions, Opinions, Beliefs and Choices" in a healthy nonjudgmental and unconditional loving manner. In short, my deficient in the value of learning about another person's perspective, displayed my unhealthy preference to be close-minded and always too focused on being Right.

My characteristics, at the time, hindered me from emulating the role of a productive unconditional loving Father Figure. Yes, "**I loss my way**" in balancing the Father Figure paramount role, as the biblical Father Figure within our home and away from the home. For these failures, I apologize to my three beautiful and lovely daughters, Cassandra, Octavia, and Jennifer.

To Crystal Smith, I would like to express my deepest apology to you because, at the time of our union, I was not aware of all my embedded unprocessed developmental adolescence and adulthood Mental Health, as well as the Physical Health Disorders and Symptoms.

Crystal Smith and I met on a rainy night in 2008, at an event in New Brunswick, New Jersey. The event was for a new aspiring young Presidential Candidate named Barack Obama. Our first glance at each other was like love at first sight. As shown by our conversation throughout that evening. Prior to leaving, we exchanged phone numbers. Two weeks later, she called. Yes, Crystal was the first one to call. The call did rekindle the magic that I felt the first time we met. Then on December 12, 2012, we married.

I will always recognize Crystal's wonderful attributes and characteristics. Characteristics that displayed her excellent in leadership skills, Father Figure Commitment, and her passion for doing things her way. Others excellent attributes were her Educational drive and having an extraordinarily strong biological family values as well as an exhibited honorable Independent.

My epiphany occurred in 2014. It allowed me to fully understand the harm that I caused to such a wonderful woman who genuinely loved me, despite all my exhibited unhealthy behavior patterns. In addition, it was then that I began to realize the notion and appreciation for a person's Individuality. Now, with an empathetic heart, I can process how individuality applies to all, that demonstrated by, our likes, wants, and needs.

Therefore, I, Octavius Lamont Brown, apologize to Crystal Smith for my inability to understand her needs, appreciate the value of her individuality, and display the Father Figure Role Model commitment throughout our marriage.

My deepest concern and another primary reason why I felt obligated to author this book. Is, once again and **for the last time,** because it took **me fifty-five years** to finally recognize that I have serious embedded unprocessed psychological Mental Health symptoms, as evidenced, unhealthy episodes of anger, arrogance and a harden Heart.

In addition, in speaking with one of my cousins in early 2021, Bishop Anthony Fisher, currently living in Charlotte, North Carolina. He said to me, after I told him about my intention to author a book is "that there are massive number of unwritten books in the graveyard." That comment will always ruminate in my thoughts.

Furthermore, Bishop Anthony Fisher comment compelled me to make a major commitment to finish writing my first book soon. In addition, I even quit my job in mid-2021 and removed distractions within my lifestyle to dedicate the year 2021, as the year that I will finish writing my first Book. So, Bishop Anthony Fisher, aka Tony, thank you for your support in helping me to author this Book.

One other hope in authoring this book is to highlight how established mature couples, over the age of twenty-five, frequently make common relationship errors. Two of those common errors are not appreciating the importance their **Individuality**. Individuality that forms the foundation of a person, prior to formation of any union. Our Individuality entitles us to explore our desired lifestyle within and outside of their home, as well as personal occupational professional aspirations. The other is the fundamental goal of the Father Figure Commitment. In relationship prior to the transition as one, there need to be a series of open one-on-one conversations about Individuality and the Father Figure Commitment.

ABOUT THE AUTHOR

Deacon Octavius Lamont Brown, MBA, MSCC, CASAC Master Level, LCADC and LPC is the Founder, CEO, and CAO of DOC OCTAVIUS MENTAL HEALTH SERVICES.

Octavius L. Brown was born on July 6, 1951, in Queens, New York and raised in the South Bronx of New York City (aka. "Boogie down Bronx"). On his sixteenth birthday, in the summer of 1967, he woke up early to gather his Birth Certificate and Social Security Card to travel to Employment Office for a job. After a quick breakfast, he walked out of Melrose Project building 681 Courtland Ave, Bronx New York to the State Employment Office, on East 149 Street off Courtland Avenue. The goal was to get a real paying hourly job. Prior to his sixteenth birthday, the only source of income was from his New York Post paper route, selling shopping bags in front of Department Stores like Hearns and Alexanders, as well as shining shoes in Bars and on the corners Third Avenue between E149 Street to East 153 Street.

Once he arrived at the State Employment Office, to his surprise, his enthusiasm was met with equal support from the man at the Employment Office. After basic verification of his documents, the man provided him with an address for him to go and apply for a Part-Time position. The job was at Melrose Pharmacy on the corner of East 153 Street and Courtland Ave. That was right across the street from his apartment building, and he was able to see the front of the store's window display from his bedroom window. The Pharmacist at the Pharmacy hired him to do their deliveries and stocking the store with their merchandises for sale. To his surprise the summer of 1967, he had achieved three part-time jobs. The main one was working at the Pharmacy, his New York Post paper route and a Summer Neighbor job that was paying $37.50 weekly. The Summer job were for teenagers that lived in the South Bronx area. The four plus hours of work assignment had youths within the neighbor clearing out abandoned houses and empty lots in Harlem and the South Bronx area of New York City.

On February 16, 1970, and for the next 35 years he worked at New York Telephone/ Verizon until retirement on June 30, 2005. His Telecommunication career entailed Technical Skills, Central Office Frame-men, then Switchmen, and Union Steward, as well as Central Office and later Outside Cable Manager.

Education: Bachelor of Science Degree in Business Management from Empire State College (June of 1995). Certificate of Biblical Foundation on May 5, 2007. He received Master of Business Administration in the Spring Semester of 2005 from Regis University. Then in May of 2010, he received his Master of Science in Christian Counseling Degree. On September 14, 2012, he received his **New York's License as a Certified Alcohol and Substance Abuse Counselor.** Then on December 14, 2012, he completed Cairn University third year Program with the Certificate of Advanced Specialization in Christian Counseling. Then on August 12, 2013, he passed the National Counselor Examination that led him to obtaining his **New Jersey License Professional Counselor and Alcohol and Drug Counselor Licenses, since 2018.**

He has over 12 years of Mental Health Clinical life experiences in personal and educational development that have provided him with excellent Clinical Skills on Assessments, Occupational Health, Sexual Abuse, Behavioral Health, Complex Trauma, Domestic Violence, Family, Parenting Therapy training.

He often reflects on how extremely blessed he is to have an extensive Managerial, Telecommunication Technical and Mental Health Clinical Skills to meet the participant's mental health needs. It is his honor to be able to give back to the community.

In closing, for over fifty-five years, Octavius lived with an Anger Management problem that was never diagnosed. Once he was able to realize the importance of Anger Management Counseling, it then helped him to discover the importance of mental health counseling and why we should never ignore the signs of unregulated emotion episodes, which is commonly defined as an Anger outburst. Once he became aware of his mental health concerns due to unprocessed and unresolved developmental years, he then developed coping skills to make healthy and productive decisions.

It is by the grace of GOD that he took the time to learn what were his physical and psychological triggers. That is evidenced by his readiness to practice ways to implement Anger Management techniques and healthy decision-making skills to reduce and better manage emotional triggers.

Printed in the United States
by Baker & Taylor Publisher Services